The Island of Cuba

ATTENTION PATRON:

This volume is too fragile for any future repair.
Please handle with great care.

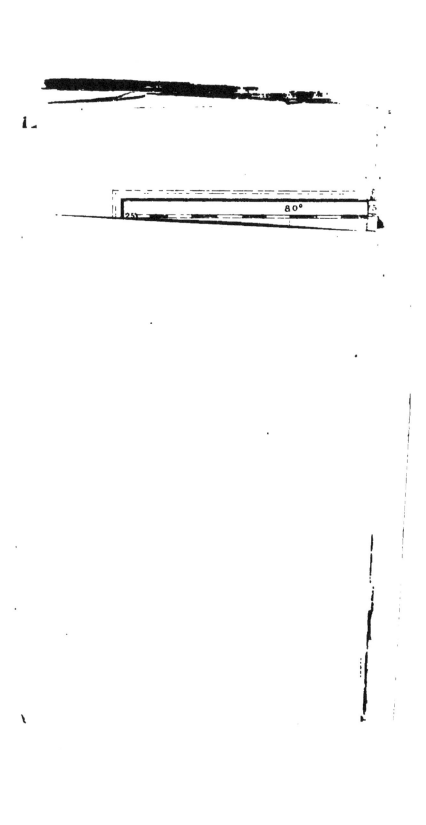

80°

25°

THE

ISLAND OF CUBA,

BY

ALEXANDER HUMBOLDT

Translated from the Spanish,

WITH

NOTES AND A PRELIMINARY ESSAY.

BY

J. S. THRASHER.

NEW YORK:

DERBY & JACKSON, 119 NASSAU STREET.

CINCINNATI:—H. W. DERBY.

1856.

W. H. TINSON, Stereotyper.   PUDNEY & RUSSELL, Printers.

TO

Che Members of the American Press

THIS WORK IS RESPECTFULLY

. DEDICATED,

IN GRATEFUL ACKNOWLEDGMENT OF THEIR SYMPATHY AND PROTECTION

IN A TIME OF PERIL,

BY THEIR OBLIGED COLABORER,

J. S. THRASHER.

PREFACE.

THAT portion of Baron Humboldt's "Personal Narrative" of his travels with Mons. Bonpland in the equinoctial regions of America, which relates to the Island of Cuba, has been published as a separate work both in the French and Spanish languages; but I believe no complete version has ever been presented in English. The following translation is from an excellent rendering of the original work into Spanish, which modestly gives only the initials of the translator; D. J. B. de V. Y. M.

I have been stimulated to undertake this labor by the oft-repeated request that I would state which is the best book on Cuba, and by the fact that a long continued residence in the island, and a study of its condition and resources, have convinced me that Baron Humboldt's work is the best that has been written on the subject.

In order to bring the information in this volume as nearly as possible down to the present time, I have added notes, which are placed in brackets in the body of the text, or without signature at the foot of the page, as seemed most conducive to a clear exposition of the present condition of Cuba. The notes of Baron Humboldt have the signature H. affixed in the following pages.

J. S. T.

New York, *December,* 1855.

CONTENTS.

———

CHAPTER III.

CLIMATE.

CHAPTER IV.

GEOGRAPHY.

CHAPTER V.

POPULATION.

CHAPTER VI..

SLAVERY.

CHAPTER VII.

RACES.

CHAPTER VIII.

SUGAR CULTURE.

CHAPTER IX.

AGRICULTURE.

CHAPTER X.

COMMERCE.

CHAPTER XI.

INTERNAL COMMUNICATIONS.

CHAPTER XII.

REVENUE.

CHAPTER XIII.

A TRIP TO TRINIDAD.

PRELIMINARY ESSAY.

An essay upon the Island of Cuba, without some treatment of the political and social questions which affect its present condition and future development, would justly be deemed an unsatisfactory and incomplete work. We do not presume to bring to the subject anything like the clear precision, and charm of thought and style, which the admirable writer and traveller, Baron Humboldt, has thrown round the production we have ventured to reproduce in the translation which follows. But we have made these questions the subject of study for several years, under new aspects which have developed themselves since Humboldt wrote, and venture to offer the result of our observations and reflections, in the hope that they may supply an existing want, and prove interesting and serviceable to the American reader.

The complete view of the population and industrial condition of Cuba, presented in the work of Baron Humboldt, renders unnecessary any further remarks

upon that subject. We shall, therefore, limit the
considerations we have to offer, to four heads, which
are: I. The Territorial; II. The Political; III. The
Industrial; and IV. The Social relations of Cuba, as
they exist at the present time.

I. The territorial relations of the Island of Cuba,
are of a more marked and permanent character than
those of any other country of limited extent in
America, and justify the Abbé Raynal's assertion
that it is " the *boulevard* of the New World." The
peculiar formation of the eastern shore of this continent, and the prevalence in the Caribbean Sea of the
trade winds, which blow with great uniformity from
the E.N.E., with a constant oceanic current running
in its general direction, from east to west, make the
narrow ocean passages, which skirt the shore of
Cuba, the natural outlets for the commerce of Venezuela, New Granada, the isthmus States of Panama,
Costa Rica, Honduras, San Salvador, and Nicaragua.

The rich and growing commerce with the countries bordering upon the Pacific Ocean, crossing the
several routes of isthmus transit, is brought by these
natural influences, under the immediate supervision
and control of the fleets that ride in safety, in the
numerous large and well-protected harbors of Cuba.
The value of the territorial advantages thus conferred
by its geographical position, must increase in the

same ratio with the increase of trade across the various isthmus routes, and every new enterprise in those regions has a direct and practical tendency to increase the moral power of whatever government rules in Cuba. The construction of the Panama railroad, at the cost of millions of dollars to the industrial resources of the United States, although of great advantage, in a pecuniary sense, to all the nations upon whose commerce it has conferred a benefit, has brought an increase of national power only to the Spanish government in Cuba, as it has brought a great increase to the tides of national wealth which must pass before its doors, and within its easy grasp. The same result must attend every increased facility of transit across the isthmus States, and every movement which shall tend to augment the products of labor within their borders, or their intercourse with the great marts lying upon the North Atlantic Ocean.

The physical geography of all the isthmus states north of Panama, and of the republic of Mexico, give to Cuba in this respect, a peculiar natural territorial relation to all those countries. Their eastern shores are wanting in those deep and capacious harbors, so necessary not only for commerce, but for the purposes of defence, while the situation of Cuba, with her numerous ports, opposite, and almost imme-

diately contiguous to their coasts, points to her as
the natural depository for their productions, and the
scene of their commercial exchanges with the rest of
the world.

This natural relation is augmented by the physical
aspect of the countries in question.   Traversed as
they are, through their whole extent, by chains of
mountains, the construction of long lines of internal
communication, which shall concentrate their trade
upon any point within their own territory, is of very
difficult and costly attainment, and Cuba thus becomes the probable channel of their future intercourse with the nations north and east of them.
Though the value of this natural connection may
now seem small, their mineral wealth, and vast
tracts of fertile soil under a genial climate, indicate
a great increase of importance at no very distant
day, under the natural development of the progress
of America.

The Gulf of Mexico, with a shore line of nearly
six thousand miles, forms almost an exact circle, the
great ocean outlet to which is through the narrow
passage running along the northern shore of Cuba,
and within a few miles of her best and strongest harbors.   This formation of the land and sea, brings the
rich mineral tribute paid by Mexico to Europe, and
the bulky products of the region drained by the Mis-

sissippi river and its tributaries, within the control
of the government of Cuba. It may close at will
the only ocean outlet those countries possess, and
thus inflict great evils upon all their industrial interests. The actual value of the commerce which that
vast region now sends through this narrow channel,
is almost beyond the power of enumeration, and the
ceaseless tide of emigration, which is pouring its
countless thousands upon the plains west of the-Mis-
sissippi, is adding steadily to its sum. However
great may be the facilities for passenger traffic, between the Atlantic and the Western States, the bulky
products of their industry, which constitute the basis
of their prosperity, must seek the markets of the
world through the lines of internal water communication and their ocean extensions. Thus every
waning year, increasing the industrial power of the
mighty West, adds a new value to the strength that
attends the geographical position of the island of
Cuba.

The territorial relations of Cuba to the isthmus
States, and to those bordering upon the Gulf of
Mexico, for purposes of defence are also of an important character. Through its peculiar location it
guards all the avenues of approach to their shores,
making an attack upon them a movement of great
difficulty and danger, while at the same time it cuts

off all hope of a safe retreat in case of reverses to
the attacking enemy. The importance of Cuba in
this respect, in its relation to the United States, is
shown in the circumstances attending the English
expedition against Louisiana, during the last war
with England. The army and fleet of Sir Edward
Packenham were concentrated at Jamaica, and in
their advance upon the United States, were compelled to sail for nearly seven hundred miles, almost
within sight from the shores of Cuba. When forced
by the battle of New Orleans to retreat, the British
fleet, with the remains of the army on board, fled to
Havana for succor and relief, and could not proceed
to Jamaica until it had remained there some time
to refit. Had Cuba at that time borne as intimate
political as it does territorial relations, to the United
States, the British fleet not only would have found
no port of refuge there, but it could never have
safely approached our shores. A similar instance
occurred in the attack by the French upon Vera
Cruz. The fleet of Prince de Joinville concentrated
at Havana before the attack, and returned there to
refit after it had captured San Juan de Ulua.

The territorial relations of Cuba to the other
islands of the Antilles, give it a marked preponderance. In area and population it exceeds all the
other islands together, while in its abundance of safe

and capacious ports it equals them. Its geographical position gives it also peculiar advantages in respect to them. With one extremity resting in undisturbed proximity upon the Continent for support, the other extends between, and in sight of St. Domingo and Jamaica, which are the only other islands of the Antilles possessing any territorial importance. Its natural resources and facility of internal communication, give to these territorial relations a power which can never be superseded by any combination of natural or acquired advantages in the other islands of the American Archipelago.

Its territorial relations to the United States, constitute probably its greatest value in the estimation of European Cabinets. The geographical formation of our Atlantic and Gulf coasts places it midway between them, enabling the power that holds Cuba, to impede at will all maritime intercourse between their ports. At the same time it is the key to the sea gates of more than twenty thousand miles of river navigation emptying into the Gulf of Mexico, the shutting of which would inflict serious injury upon every interest connected with the great valley of the Mississippi. The evil effects of such an untoward event, would be felt not only by the industrial pursuits of the great and increasing States in that region, but also by the manufacturing and com-

mercial interests of the North and East, to which
their important markets would be closed by the
double operation of impeded intercourse, and the
diminished ability of the West to consume the products and fabrics of the East, consequent upon their
inability to dispose of their own surplus productions.

The territorial relations of the island of Cuba to
the United States, have also a great importance in
another branch of their domestic economy. It constitutes more than one-half of a bar of foreign territory, laying directly over the most important lines
of transit between the Atlantic and Pacific States of
the Confederacy, across or through which must pass
the greater portion of the trade and intercourse between those sections, and of the armament and means
for military defence of the Pacific States, if they
would avoid the uncertain delays and dangers incident to the route round Cape Horn. The traffic by
the isthmus routes, between the ports of New York
and San Francisco alone, is now of greater importance and value than our foreign trade with any one
hation, Great Britain not excepted. The value of
treasure and merchandise transported by these routes
exceeds annually one hundred millions of dollars, while
more than one hundred thousand passengers throng
them, giving employment to nearly one-half the
ocean steam tonnage registered in the United States.

This bar of foreign territory over-lying these important lines of transit, extends from Cape Catoche, in Yucatan, which is the eastern point of Mexico, to the island of Porto Rico, a distance of fourteen hundred miles; and, under the geographical necessities of trade and travel, may be said, without any distortion of language, to lie immediately between the Atlantic and the Pacific States. Through this bar of foreign territory there are but three passages open to commerce, all of which are in possession, or under the immediate control of, European powers. The most western of these is the narrow passage between Cape Catoche and the western end of Cuba, forming the southern outlet to the Gulf of Mexico, and which can be approached from the Atlantic ports, only by first passing through the channel between the north coast of Cuba and the reefs of Florida. This passage lies about one hundred and fifty miles leeward from Havana.

The passage next eastward is the channel between the eastern end of Cuba and the western extremity of St. Domingo. It is about forty miles wide at the narrowest part, having the harbors of St. Jago and Guantanamo, in Cuba, on one side, Gonave and Port au Prince, in Hayti, on the other, and Jamaica lying directly across its southern outlet. These two are those most frequented in our intercourse between the

Atlantic and the Pacific States. The other passage
is the narrow channel between the eastern end of St.
Domingo and the island of Porto Rico, and is
under the immediate control of the powers holding
those two islands, being commanded by the bay of
Samana, in St. Domingo, and the harbors in the
Spanish island of Porto Rico.

Of the territory comprised in this long extent of
country, Cuba, being one-half, and Porto Rico, one-
tenth, belong to Spain, the government of which can
barely be said to be an independent power; while
St. Domingo, comprising about one-third, is held by
the negro dynasty of Hayti and the mongrel government of Dominica, neither of which has a self-ruled
policy. Jamaica, in possession of Great Britain,
laps the contiguous extremities of the two greater
islands. Cuba alone, of the Antilles, possesses sufficient territorial power to keep these passages open
to our commerce, and to guarantee their safety.
These territorial relations of that island, possessing as
they do an important bearing upon all the neighboring
countries, and conferring a moral power upon the government that holds it, are the subject of solicitude to
the governments of Western Europe, and seem worthy of the watchful care of the statesmen of America.

II. The political relations of Cuba, strictly speaking, are those of the crown of Spain, to which it is

subject; but the condition of the two countries is so distinct, that it has given rise to natural political necessities and relations, or affinities, on the part of Cuba, which are separate from, and not unfrequently opposed to those of the Spanish monarchy; the one being wholly a European power, while the other, through her great productions and commerce, has natural relations of a purely American character.

The essential political interests of the island are antagonistic to those of the mother country. While the Cortes and the crown have frequently declared that Cuba does not form an integral part of the Spanish monarchy, but must be governed by special laws not applicable to Spain, and persist in ruling her under the erroneous and unjust European colonial system, the growing wealth and increasing intelligence of the Cubans, lead them to aspire to some share in the elimination of the political principles under which their own affairs shall be administered.

A like antagonism exists in the economical relations of the two countries. While the people of Cuba are not averse to the raising of such revenue as may be required for the proper wants of the State, in the administration of which they may participate, they complain with a feeling of national pride, that fiscal burdens of the most onerous kind are laid upon them for the expressed purpose of

advancing interests which are in every sense opposed
to their own. Thus Spain imposes taxes to support
a large army and navy, the principal object of which
is to prevent any expression of the public will on the
part of the people of Cuba. Another class of impositions have for their object the diversion of the
trade of Cuba to channels which shall increase the
profits of the agriculturalists, and mariners of Spain,
without regard to the interests of the people of the
island. Whenever any of these burdens become so
oppressive, or ruinous to the island, that the court
cannot avoid taking cognizance of the complaints of
the people, the necessity that it must be replaced by
some new tax, which shall immediately equal it in
product to the revenue, is made the immutable condition of relief. In a word, the increase of the revenue, and the advance of the -industrial interests of
the people of Spain, are the guiding principles in
the political economy of the present government of
Cuba.

The civil administration of Cuba is of the same
antagonistic character. We are relieved from
extending our remarks on this point, by the full
elucidation of the subject in the "Essay upon the
political state, &c., of the Island of Cuba," published
by General José de ·la Concha, in Spain, after. his
return from the post of Captain-General of the

island. The propositions sustained by General Concha are, that "The prosperity of Cuba is not due to the so-called laws of the Indies; nor does it prove the social welfare of the island; nor the excellence of its government." The result of this evil political system has been to create a feeling of dissatisfaction among the people of Cuba, and a direful determination on the part of the government, which is thus expressed by General Cañedo in his farewell address to the people of Cuba, on resigning the command of the island to General Pezuela, in December 1853.

"Remain then impassive in the love which you profess to our august queen, and to the mother country; remain obedient to the supreme government and to the authority which represents it, and never forget that the very existence and name of Cuba depends upon its continuing to be a Spanish possession."

The political relations of Cuba towards the other continental nations of Europe, partake of the passive antagonism inherent in the communities of America; but as this is entirely absorbed by its submission to Spain, these relations exhibit only the character of those of the Spanish crown.

With Great Britain a severe contest has been carried on for several years, during which the mother country, up to a certain period, defended the interests

2

of her colony.   The countervailing policy of France
in the Spanish peninsula, more than any other circumstance, enabled Spain to resist the demands of
England; but the advent of Louis Napoleon, and his
hearty union with the British cabinet in a policy,
which the Earl of Clarendon describes as affecting
the policy of those nations in both hemispheres,
changed the relative position of those governments -
toward Spain.   England claimed the right, under
treaty stipulations, to interfere in the domestic affairs
of Cuba, and as this claim and the attendant negotia-
tions involve some of the most important questions
relative to the future of Cuba, we give the following
extracts from the official correspondence on the subject.   They will best exhibit the relative positions
and aims of the two governments, and perhaps throw
some light upon a matter which is still involved in
the obscurity of diplomatic intercourse.   The possible
stipulations of Spain with England on this subject;
have awakened the liveliest alarm in Cuba, and have
been the subject of much warm discussion in this
country.

In 1841 England endeavored to establish by treaty
a British tribunal in Cuba, with power to decide the
status of the negroes making application to it.   Lord
Aberdeen, in a dispatch of 31st December 1843, to
Mr. Bulwer, then British Minister in Spain, holds the

following language in relation to this attempt, and its temporary abandonment.

"In 1841, the draft of a Convention was transmitted to Madrid, by which it was proposed to institute, by the aid of British functionaries, an examination into the titles by which the slave population of Cuba is held in servitude. Encouraged by the novel appearance of good faith on the part of the government of Cuba, as it was then administered, her Majesty's government admitted the weight of certain objections raised against that proposal by the government at Madrid, and forbore for the time to press it."[1]

The objections here alluded to, were the remonstrances from Cuba, which were couched in the strongest language. On the first allusion to the subject by the press in Spain, the Junta de Fomento of Havana sent to the court a protest signed by Count Villanueva (the intendant of the island), as president of that body, which, after eloquently depicting the results of that measure to Cuba, says:—

"It is not to be presumed that any white man will be disposed to submit to so hard a fate. They will all prefer to emigrate to foreign countries to earn

[1] Report on the Slave Trade, laid before Parliament, 1853, pp. 69-70.

their livelihood and save the lives of their children, if they do not previously adopt the course which a state of desperation would prescribe." * * *

* * * "There has been but one feeling or opinion since the arrival of the publications in question from Madrid, which is, that the island would be irrecoverably lost by it to the mother country, and to its inhabitants, who would prefer any extreme to the calamity of sacrificing their fortunes, endangering their lives, and remaining in a state of subordination to the negroes."[1]

This "Draft of a Convention" was sent to Cuba by the Regency of Spain, for consultation, and produced the most urgent remonstrances from the municipal authorities of Havana, the Junta de Fomento, and other public bodies, and from many eminent citizens to whom it was submitted by the local authorities. Their language was uniform and bold, the Ayuntamiento of Havana declaring that if the Convention were signed by Spain, it would be productive of a bloody revolution in Cuba. These representations induced England to forbear. for a time.

In 1850 and 1851, these demands were again

---

[1] Correspondence on the Slave Trade, published by order of the House of Commons, 1841, Class B, p. 286.

pressed by England with great energy and warmth, and strenuously resisted by Spain. On the 23d March, 1851, Señor Bertran de Lis writes to Lord Howden:

"But it seems impossible that the well-known perspicuity of the Cabinet of London should have overlooked in its turn the immense responsibility imposed upon the queen's government by the present circumstances of the Spanish Antilles, and the stringent duty in which it is placed, of proceeding with the greatest prudence and circumspection, in all matters which may exercise either directly or indirectly any influence upon the social and political situation of those colonies.

"You are aware of the dangers by which these colonies are menaced. You know that for the prevention of these dangers, for the consolidation of the security and preservation of its transatlantic possessions, her majesty's government, hitherto, unfortunately, reduced to its own means, cannot as yet rely upon the decided protection of its most important allies." [1]

The moment was opportune for England, and she did not hesitate to take advantage of it. General Lopez was at that time preparing in this country his

---

[1] Report on the Slave Trade, &c., 1853, p. 72.

second expedition to Cuba; and Spain feared the
possible loss of her colony. In the midst of these
anxieties Lord Palmerston writes to Lord Howden,
the British minister at Madrid:

[Extract.]   FOREIGN OFFICE, 10th July, 1851.

"The Spanish government will do well to consider
that if such a course of proceeding shall continue,
the people of this country, instead of looking with
displeasure at attempts which may be made to sever
Cuba from the Spanish monarchy, may be led to
view with satisfaction the accomplishment of an
event, which, in consequence of the conduct of the
Spanish colonial authorities, will have become the
only means of putting an end to the commission of
crimes which the Spanish crown solemnly bound itself, many years ago, utterly and for ever to prevent
any Spanish subject from committing."[1]

LORD PALMERSTON TO LORD HOWDEN.

[Extract.]   FOREIGN OFFICE, 7th August, 1851.

"Her majesty's government deem it due to the
frankness which ought to characterize the intercourse
of friendly governments, to let the Spanish government know, that if, as seems to be the case, the government of Madrid is unable to cause its subordinate

---

[1] Published dispatches.

officers in Cuba to carry into execution the treaty engagements of the Spanish crown for the suppression of the slave-trade, and to enforce the laws promulgated by the crown of Spain in execution of those engagements, the British government must deem itself obliged to take the matter into its own hands, and to have recourse to such measures in relation to it as may appear to her majesty's government best calculated to accomplish the purpose in view." [1]

These threatenings were replied to by the Marquis de Miraflores on the part of Spain, in a firm tone. On the 19th of August, he wrote to Lord Howden :—

"If by any unfortunate combination of circumstances, or perhaps in consequence of an inconsiderate zeal, or from any motive whatsoever, an undue interference on the part of the commanders of the new naval forces in matters of maritime or internal jurisdiction of the island of Cuba, were to give rise to some conflict with the authorities of that island; if in this or any way, a new element of disturbance were added to the numerous ones, which, in spite of the government of the United States, are fostered against that island by American pirates, in combination with some disloyal natives of Cuba, her majesty's government declares at once, that after repulsing with all the

[1] Published dispatches.

energy in its power any intrusion of that kind, it will
hold the cabinet of London responsible for the fatal
consequences which might therefrom ensue to Spanish domination, under the critical circumstances
under which it is now placed in the West Indies.
And finally, that should the conflicts above alluded
to take place, the Spanish government would not
hesitate to appeal to the decision of the whole of
Europe, trusting that public opinion, even in the ever
loyal and enlightened English nation itself, would
justly appreciate whether the conduct of the British
government would have been such as the government
of the queen, my august sovereign, has a right to
expect from a power which calls itself the friend and
ally of Spain, and even consistent with what was
required by the interests of England itself." [1]

On the 11th of September, Lord Palmerston replied
to the Marquis of Miraflores, disclaiming all wish to
violate the rights of Spain, but at the same time
desiring to come to a plain understanding with the
government at Madrid, and to make that government
comprehend that "Great Britain will no longer consent to be baffled;" and throwing upon the government of Spain any consequences that may arise.
During this correspondence, the Marquis de Miraflo-

---

[1] Published dispatches.

res skillfully availed himself of an apparent contradiction in the arguments and recomendations of England, to which Lord Palmerston replies:—

"With reference to that passage in M. Miraflores' note, in which he states that the Spanish government cannot understand how her majesty's government can seriously recommend a measure which would prove very injurious to the natives of Cuba, when they also recommend that the Spanish government should conciliate the affections of those Cubans, I have to instruct your lordship to observe to M. de Miraflores that the slaves of Cuba form a large portion, and by no means an unimportant one, of the population of Cuba; and that any steps taken to provide for their emancipation would, therefore, as far as the black population are concerned, be quite in unison with the recommendation made by her majesty's government; that measures should be adopted for contenting the people of Cuba, with a view to secure the connexion-between that island and the Spanish crown; and it must be evident that if the negro population of Cuba were rendered free, that fact would create a most powerful element of resistance to any scheme for annexing Cuba to the United States, where slavery still exists." [1]

[1] Published dispatches.

2*

This correspondence, which was continued during · the succeeding year, did not attain the desired result, and in December, 1852, Lord Palmerston, in a dispatch to Lord Howden, thus forcibly depicts the reasons which animate the Spanish government to resist the demands of England.

. "First, in order to afford income to a number of ill-paid public officers, or to appointed favorites, by means of bribes given by slave-traders; and

"Secondly, for the purpose of retaining a hold upon the island; because it is thought at Madrid, that as long as there is in Cuba a large number of negroes, the white population will cling to the mother country for protection against the black race.

"But both these motives are founded in error, for it can never be the interest of a government to demoralize its own officers, and to accustom them to violate the law; and a mother country will have but a feeble hold of a colony, if the strongest tie which connects them, is the fear on the part of the planter of an insurrection of the negroes.

"It is obvious that protection against such danger might be found by other means, and in other quarters; by the suppression of the slave trade, which many Cuban proprietors desire; *or by annexation*

' to some other State, for which scheme there are not wanting partisans in Cuba."[1]

These extracts show the antagonistic positions held by the governments of Spain and Great Britain to the close of the year 1852, and afford a clear insight into the aims of the ' latter, in regard to the political and social relations of Cuba. In the beginning of 1853, these positions were unchanged, and England continued to press her demands with unabated vigor. This is evident from the following dispatches :

LORD JOHN RUSSELL TO LORD HOWDEN.

[Extract.]   " FOREIGN OFFICE, January 31, 1853.

"Your lordship may be assured, that however friendly the councils of her majesty may be to Spain, whatever may be the interest of this country not to see Cuba in the hands of any other power than Spain, yet, in the eyes of the people of this country, the destruction of a trade which conveys the natives of Africa to become slaves in Cuba, will furnish a large compensation for such a transfer. For such an exhibition of public feeling the government of Spain should be prepared."[2]

[1] London Daily News, 31st December, 1852.
[2] Report on the Slave Trade, 1853—p. 195.

CONDE DE ALCOY TO LORD HOWDEN.

[Extract.]   "MADRID, February 9, 1853.

"Her majesty's government has seen with deep
regret the hint made by your lordship as to the effect
which the supposed increase of the slave-trade is
likely to produce on the opinion of England, with
regard to the manner of viewing the fact of the
island of Cuba being taken possession of by another
power; and I assure your lordship that what on this
subject is particularly painful to her majesty's government, and even more regretable than any considerations affecting the immediate interests of Spain,
is the melancholy reflection that the change of opinion in England, which your lordship anticipates,
would be a triumph for the partisans of force, and a
defeat for the upholders of right; because from the
moment in which it should be declared that, for more
or less plausible reasons, although not connected
with the questions of right, it is lawful to look with
indifference at the spoliation of one nation by
another nation, the subversion of all principles, and
the oblivion of the law of nations, on which the
peace of the world is resting, would then be sanc-
tioned.   *   *   *

"At all events, the government, who knows the
loyalty, and the noble feelings of the Spanish nation,

is well aware that, should the case arrive for it to defend her right, this nation will do her duty as she has done on former occasions, without counting the elements of resistance, and relying only on God and the sanctity of her cause, and on her constancy and valor."[1]

This position of Spain towards England, was soon after changed for one of complete harmony with regard to the social and political relations of Cuba, and it is somewhat remarkable that the change in the position of the Spanish government was so sudden, and unexpected by England, that conflicting dispatches were written on the same day to each other, by the secretary for foreign affairs in London, and the British minister at Madrid. On the 16th of March, 1853, the Earl of Clarendon writes to Lord Howden that the position of Spain " endangers the friendly relations between the two countries;"[2] and on the same day Lord Howden writes to the Earl of Clarendon, that " the Spanish government has agreed to a settlement of a question which has long been a matter of painful discussion and dispute."[3] What the conditions of this settlement were, can only be partially conjectured from subsequent

---

[1] Report on the Slave Trade, p. 196.

[2] Report on the Slave Trade, 1853—p. 196. [3] Do. p. 74.

events, and from the measures taken by Spain in
Cuba. Lord John Russell stated in Parliament, on
the 4th of May following, that they were satisfactory
to England.

Coincident with this arrangement between England and Spain, there are two remarkable statements
made by British statesmen. On the occasion of the
rejection by the United States, of the proposition
made by England and France, to enter into a tripar-
tite treaty relative to Cuba, Lord John Russell
directs the British minister at Washington to say to
the American secretary of state :

"Finally, while fully admitting the right of the
United States to reject the proposal made by Lord
Malmesbury, and Mons. de Turgot, Great Britain
must at once resume her entire liberty, and upon any
occasion that may call for it, be free to act either
singly or in conjunction with other powers, as to her
may seem fit."

Lord Clarendon, while secretary for foreign
affairs, subsequently made in Parliament this celebrated announcement relative to the united policy
of England and France.

"I will further add that the union between the
two governments has not been confined to the Eas-

tern question. The happy accord and good understanding between France and England, have been
extended beyond the Eastern policy to the policy
affecting all parts of the world, and I am heartily
rejoiced to say, that there is no portion of the two
hemispheres with regard to which the policy of the
two countries, however heretofore antagonistic, is not
now in entire harmony."

The foregoing extracts, with the subsequent measures taken by Spain in Cuba, render it evident that
the political relations of the island to England, which
were for a long time the subject of warm discussion,
have experienced a radical change. The conduct of
the British naval commanders in the mid-American
waters last winter, sustain this view. As the effects
of this change, and the consequent measures taken
by the Spanish government in Cuba, relate more
particularly to the social relations of that island, we
shall consider them under that head.

The political relations of Cuba to the republics of
Spanish America, are of the most limited character.
Havana was for a long time the centre of the operations by Spain against her revolted colonies, and
became the refuge of her troops, when they were
driven from the continent. The few years that
have elapsed since the recognition of the independ-

ence of those countries by Spain, have not sufficed
to create any important political relations, between
them, to which their opposing systems of government
are also averse.   Within a few years the queen-
dowager of Spain, Maria Cristina, has maintained a
private agent at Havana, who has been connected
with intrigues in Mexico, and other places, with the
supposed object of placing a Spanish prince on an
American throne.   These movements, however, have
been of little importance.   The community of language, customs, and religion between Cuba and the
republics of Spanish America, together with their
relative geographical positions, indicate a probable
political affinity whenever the axioms of public policy
which now rule in Cuba, shall have been changed.

The political relations of Cuba with the other
islands of the Antilles, have been very slight until
within a short time.   For many years Spain did not
recognize the black empire of Hayti, and held little
intercourse with Dominica.   Lately a treaty has
been made with Soulouque and a diplomatic agent,
sent to Hayti, to act in conjunction with those of
England and France.   Existing circumstances exhibit a probable complication of these relations, at
no very distant day.   The advancing age of Soulouque, combined with the absence of a direct male
heir to his crown, and the intrigues for the succes-

sion, may soon create a state of affairs in Hayti in which the powers of western Europe, always so ready to mingle in questions of territorial difficulty, or of dynasty, may feel themselves called upon to interfere. Any infringement of the rights of a subject of either crown may form a pretext, and a cover for political designs, as we have seen in late occurrences in the Dominican republic, where a pretended infraction of individual rights, enabled them to prevent the completion of a treaty between that republic and the United States.

The political relations of Cuba with the United States constitute, in a great measure, those of Spain with this country. They have been marked with many cases of irritated feeling, arising in most part from the wrong application of general principles to private cases, by ignorant and irresponsible officials. All the exponents of Spanish public policy trace the loss of her rich American possessions to the evil example of the United States; and from this they deduce a necessity of resistance to every principle or precept, that in any way assimilates to the American theories; and this necessity, they think, can be fully complied with, only by a constant opposition to the interests of such American citizens as commerce, or any other cause, may bring within the sphere of their power. The Spanish press in Cuba also strives to impress upon the public mind the belief that a war of races exists, and that wherever the American Saxon has prevailed, the Spaniards and and their descendants have been despoiled and driven out.   ·

Influenced in a great measure by these ideas, we have seen repeated instances of abuse of power by the subordinate officials in the island, exercised upon American citizens and consuls; and on some occasions by the superior ones, when such abuse was supposed to produce an advantageous political effect in Cuba. This disposition on the part of the Spanish officers towards the United States and their citizens, has been fostered by the marked difference exhibited between the policy of the European powers and that of our own government, in regard to the rights of their subjects and citizens abroad. Whenever a subject of any of the prominent powers of Europe complains to the respresentative of his government of an infringement of his rights, his relation of the facts of the case is assumed by the representative to be the correct one, and immediate action is taken; and not unfrequently followed by an exhibition of force to compel respect, or restitution. In all such cases the representative receives the public sanction and support of his own government, even if he has acted inconsiderately; reproof for over-zeal being a subject of private administration. Unfortunately for our own citizens abroad, our government, conscious of its own respect for the rights of the foreigner here, assumes that every other government is animated by the same feeling, and has pursued a system of international intercourse the reverse of that followed by European governments;—inquiry being substituted for belief, and delay for action. Thus the wrong is often consummated, and submitted to by the citizen, because the seeking of redress is more ruinous to him than submission, and the affair is forgotten,—no administration being anxious to assume and correct the omissions of former ones. If any representative abroad embroils himself with the subordinates of a foreign power, in seeking redress for our citizens, his communications to the cabinet at Washington remain unanswered, and he is not unfrequently abandoned to the degrading sense of having urged an unsustained demand. For the support of these assertions, we do not hesitate to appeal to every one of our citizens, who has been in public position abroad as a representative of the United States.

These circumstances have tended to complicate our political relations with Cuba, for the nature of the Spanish character has been so orientalized, by the seven hundred years of Moorish dominion in

Spain, that a Spaniard generally respects only those
whose power he fears; and being released from all
fear of that of the United States, the conduct of the
subordinate Spanish officials towards our citizens and
representatives, is uniformly one of disrespect, covered with a thin mask of great politeness. Thus has
arisen the long list of insults to consuls, and outrages
upon private citizens, presented by the history of our
relations with Cuba; and which, through each succeeding neglect, has so increased, that no administration has yet been found with sufficient nerve to
open the whole subject.

III. The industrial relations of Cuba are exhibited
in detail in the pages of the following work, and a
few general remarks are all that are required here.
The nature of her soil, climate, and labor, peculiarly
adapt her to the production of sugar, coffee, and
tobacco, and to the cultivation of these three staples
her industry has been mainly directed. Under these
circumstances, an untrammelled commerce with
other countries is as necessary to her social existence,
as it is for the advance of her public wealth. The
meats and grains for the subsistence, as well as the
fabrics for the use of the inhabitants, must be obtained from other countries through the medium of
commercial exchanges. In conducting these, the
care and intelligence of individuals directly inter-

ested in the result of each private enterprise, are better able to attain an advantageous result to each adventure, than the wisest legislation can possibly be; and it is the aggregate of individual profits that constitutes the public gain, and the welfare of the State. The commerce of Cuba, therefore, would be most advantageously conducted, if left to the natural promptings of individual profit and loss. A different economical theòry, however, prevails with the government of Cuba, and restrictive laws modify her industrial action in a manner that produces a large positive loss to her.

Her natural exchanges with Spain are the products of her own labor, in return for the fruits of Andalusia, and the wines of Catalonia. The existing laws, however, compel her to purchase in Spain all the flour consumed in Cuba, at a cost fifty per cent. greater than she could obtain it in nearer markets, if free to seek them; while the same obstacles force her to import in Spanish ships, a large portion of the products brought from other countries, at a much greater cost for freight than if her merchants could employ those who would perform the service at the lowest rate. Thus, for a valuable portion of her trade, she is forced to employ two sets of ships; one to bring the linens and cottons from the looms of

Europe to her ports, and another, which comes empty
to her shores, to convey the return cargoes of sugar
and other productions. Without the existing system
of differential duties in favor of Spanish bottoms,
the vessels which now come to Cuba in ballast from
Europe, would supply all the wants of the trade,
and the costly employment of a large number of
Spanish vessels could be dispensed with.

The industrial relations of Cuba with the northern
nations of Europe, are principally confined to the
exchange of her products for their linen and cotton
fabrics, glass, and iron ware.

England loans her the capital to build her railways,
and the improvements made in the arts and sciences
in France, are eagerly studied, and readily adopted
by the people of Cuba, particularly in everything
relating to their own immediate pursuits.

The industrial relations of Cuba with the United
States have been of a more important character, and
have had more influence in her material progress,
than those with any other country. In the dawning
years of her prosperity, she found here the food and
lumber for the supply of her agricultural industry;
the articles of use or luxury desired for the comfort
of her people; and, in no small degree, the skill and
capital for the development of commerce, and the

mechanic arts in her ports. During many years her trade with this country exceeded that with all other nations.

There are, probably, no two separate countries whose industrial relations are so completely reciprocal, as those of Cuba and the United States. Producing staples that enter into constant general use in this country, the natural wants of her people afford a market for the products of every section of the Union. The forests, fisheries, manufactures, and shipping of New England; the farmers, dairymen, miners, and handworkers of the middle States; the lumber-men, naval stores, and rice-growers of the South; and the meats and grains of the West, all find an appropriate exchange in the markets of Cuba. An adverse fiscal system, aided by our own unwise retaliatory acts of 1832-3, have changed the course of a large portion of this trade, and retarded its general increase.

The cotton and linen manufactures of Europe are consumed in Cuba to the value of five millions of dollars annually, a large portion of which might be supplied by the better and cheaper products of American looms. In the same manner we find that unequal fiscal impositions change the natural current of other branches of trade, and that flour, instead of being purchased in the cheapest mart in the world,

is sought on the other side of the Atlantic; that olive
oil of the most inferior quality is enabled to compete
largely with lard for domestic purposes; and that of
forty millions pounds of meats imported, less than
three millions, or about seven per cent. only, is
imported from the United States: while butter and
pork, being subject to an equality of fiscal exactions,
are imported to the extent of more than ninety per
cent. from this country.

The proximity of Cuba to the United States, and
the constant and frequent intercourse between them,
have been productive of the happiest effect upon the
industry of the island. Her infant coastwise commerce found, in our small vessels, a ready supply for
its needs; and her steam navigation received its first
impulse and subsequent growth from our own. The
erection of machinery, and the application of steam
power to labor in all parts of Cuba, have also been,
in no small degree, the result of this proximity; and
the influence of these, and many concurrent relations,
has been felt in every throb of her industrial system.

The industrial relations of Cuba with Spanish
America have been injuriously affected by political
causes which have nearly destroyed a once profitable
trade with the ports on the Gulf of Mexico, and the
Caribbean sea. The most important branch of commerce with them is the trade in jerked beef brought

from Buenos Ayres. It is not a reciprocal trade, for the countries of La Plata consume a very small amount of Cuban products; but is the fruit of the present fiscal system of the island, the greater duties upon the meats of North America forcing the consumer to seek a supply from the inferior products of the plains of South America.

The true relation of Cuba, or rather of its chief port, Havana, to Spanish America, is indicated by Baron Humboldt, in comparing it to the relation of New York to the United States. This natural connection has been severed by the wars of independence in Mexico, and South America, and almost annihilated by the long continued obstinacy of Spain, in refusing to acknowledge the independence of her former colonies. Speaking of the early years of the present century, Baron Humboldt says, "Havana purchases in foreign marts much larger quantities of goods than are needed for her own consumption, exchanging her colonial products for the fabrics of Europe, and selling them again at Vera Cruz, Truxillo, Laguaira, and Carthagena." The proximity and frequent communication of Havana with the United States and Europe, should have made her the medium not only for the interchanges of commerce with Spanish America, but also for those of politics, science, art, and literature.

8

When the former Spanish colonies were severed
from Havana, they were in a great measure deprived
of a necessary connection with the advancing civilization of Europe and America, the rays of which,
gathered as it were in a focus by the world-wide commerce of that city, would have become assimilated,
and adapted there, to the spirit and needs of her sister communities, reflecting thence upon them, to their
constantly increasing advantage and enlightenment.
The elements of that natural relation with Spanish
America, still exist in the admirable geographical
position of Havana, in the community of language
and religious faith, and in the reciprocal necessities
of the people.   Here we may find the key to the true
theory of the regeneration of Spanish America; for
we cannot suppose that the extension of American
institutions, and of our theories of freedom, and self-
government over those countries, involve the annihilation of the Spanish race in America.

IV. The social condition and relations of Cuba
have been influenced and modified by her insular
position, and by her political connection with Spain.
To the first of these is, probably, to be traced the
cause that her population is composed in a great
measure of two unmixed races—the European white
and the African black; and to the second, the reason
that, notwithstanding a community of origin and

language, there is little social affinity between her population and the Spanish American nations of the continent. In contemplating the present social condition of Cuba, we should not forget the origin and causes of the principles and laws upon which it is based.

The early settlers of Cuba and of South America were fearless adventurers seeking for gold. The native races of the Antilles soon melted away under the hardships imposed upon them by their new task-masters, and these, cavaliers and hardy men-at-arms, were unfitted to till the soil, or pursue the peaceful avocations so necessary to the welfare of every community. The disappearance of the indigenous races gave rise to a great social necessity in the new settlements. "Send us at once," say the Spanish officers in Cuba, in 1534, to the emperor, "send us at once the seven thousand negroes, that they may become inured to labor, before the Indians cease to exist; otherwise the inhabitants cannot sustain themselves, nor the government detain any one here, for with the new tidings from Peru, all desire to leave."

This social necessity gave birth to negro slavery in America; but the new institution made little progress until the humanitarian arguments, which we find again brought forward now for its destruction, were brought to its aid. Las Casas, bishop of

Chiapas, moved by the deepest compassion for the native races, urged, upon the ground of humanity, the substitution of African slaves for the natives in the labor of the new communities. The hardships of the poor Indian were dwelt upon with the same fervor and zeal, the same heedless inconsistency, that characterizes the appeals of the humanitarians of the present day in behalf of the negro, and the conscience of Europe gave an energetic impulse to the new institution. Thus did a fallacious sentiment of humanity give life to the new social system in America, and work a change in the material condition of man throughout the world, widely different from that anticipated for it by its early apostles.

The cultivation, in the New World, of the so-called colonial staples, has produced effects far surpassing those of all the gold discoveries in the world, from those of Cibao to those of California and Australia. Not only have the looms and the world-wide commerce of Europe, drawn their richest springs of life from the cultivation of cotton and sugar by the slaves of America, but a revolution has been effected by it, in the clothing and food of man everywhere, that has wrought the happiest effects upon his social, moral, and hygienic condition. The humbler classes of the present age would deem it a hardship to be confined to the bacon and beer breakfasts of the

sumptuous Queen Elizabeth, and millions now re-
joice in the once highly-esteemed luxury of stockings.

It has become orthodox with modern humanitarians to question the humanity of the theory of
Las Casas. If we could have an impartial view of
the condition of the great mass of negroes in Africa,
of their social and military slavery from the earliest
ages, subject to the sway of barbarous native chiefs,
it might be found that his argument in favor of the
change from a savage to a civilized master, was not so
inconclusive as is now supposed; and that the step
itself was not so cruel as it has been, and still is
painted. But if we doubt the humanity of the social
theories of Las Casas, and the humanitarians of the
sixteenth century, what verdict may not posterity
accord to those of Wilberforce and the humanitarians of the nineteenth century, when it contemplates
the results of their social experiments in St. Domingo,
Jamaica, and the other islands of the American
Archipelago.

The two unmixed races exist in Cuba, under a
social organization in which the inferior is subject to
the superior race, to the manifest material and moral
advantage of both. The material condition of the
inferior or slave race, is not that degraded and suffering state of deprivation, which the reasoners upon
the abstract question of slavery assume it to be. On

the contrary, the relation of master and slave is one
of mutual dependence, and creates ties between
them which do not exist in countries where the two
races live in a state of civil equality. The feelings
of affection incident to an intimate and continued
intercourse from the cradle to the grave, are not
interfered with or broken by the existence of separate interests. Though the slave is bound to reside
with and labor for his master, this does not infer that
his whole time and strength is consumed in bringing
profit to his owner. It is true the general direction
of his labors lies with his master, yet the slave in
America is able to devote a much larger portion of
his time and strength, to his own individual comfort
and pleasure, than is the manufacturing or agricultural laborer, who is not a freeholder, in those communities where slavery does not exist. Not only are
his present wants supplied, in return for his labor,
but he has no future of age and poverty to provide
for, or to fear. His material condition is thus one
of comparative happines, (and all happiness is comparative), and this is further improved by the insti-
gations of interest with his master, and by that
friendly sentiment toward all who are dependent
upon us, or upon whom we have conferred a favor,
which is innate to the human heart. The possession
of power, or control by the slaveholder, over the

labor of his slaves, does not make him a tyrant, but rather does it give him a feeling of stronger affinity with them, apart from that of interest, and creates in his breast those friendly ties which every human bosom experiences for its dependents.

The moral condition of the slave is also benefited by his relation with his master. Every individual is brought into an intimate connection with a better society, and example, than is afforded him by his own class exclusively, and the faculty of imitation, which is much stronger in the negro than that of origination, stimulates him to imitate his superior, rather than his equal. At the same time the exercise of the control of a superior intelligence over his social intercourse, and moral deportment, are productive of a state of morals which will compare most favorably with that of the lower classes under a different social organization. A respect for the laws, and for the rights of others is thereby inculcated, and the religious sentiment is developed to a degree never found in the free negro, and seldom in the same relative class in other communities. Pauperism never exists among slaves, and great crimes are much more rare among them than among the lower classes in free States.

It is under this social organization, that Cuba has risen to that condition of material prosperity which

she exhibits to the world, and that is so clearly set
forth in the following work of Baron Humboldt.
This material prosperity indicates a state of social
welfare, as does public decay argue a state of private
or individual suffering.   Before we proceed to examine the new measures which Spain proposes to introduce into the legislation of Cuba, let us contemplate
the condition of those communities, where, under
similar circumstances of climate and population, the
new social theories have been carried into practice.

Of the social condition of the negro community of
Hayti we have few means of judging, and these are
offered only by transient visitors.   Its government
does not attempt to attain any social statistics, and
the evidences presented by the material aspects of
the country, lead to the most lamentable conjectures
as to the actual condition of the inhabitants.   It is
generally admitted that they have relapsed far
toward a state of barbarism, and that the dark
practices of *fetish* worship, and heathenism, are
rapidly extinguishing there the light of the genial
precepts of Christianity.

Jamaica affords us better means for contemplating
the results attending the experiment of the civil
equality of the black with the white race, where the
numbers of the former preponderate, and those, too,
of a character that does not admit of doubt.   From

"A report of the Central Board of Health of Jamaica," in 1852, printed by order of the Assembly of that island, we make the following extracts:

"Generally speaking, the towns and villages are straggling, and cover a large space of ground in proportion to the number of houses. The streets are often crooked and irregular, * * * for the most part narrow, unpaved, flat or even concave, and without any provision for foot passengers; too frequently they become the receptacle for all sorts of filth and dirt." —Page 98.

"Yards * * * which after a rain send forth streams of the most horrible description; numbers of dilapidated and falling houses, useless for all habitable purposes, ruined walls and remnants of fences, together with unenclosed sites of pulled-down houses, covered with filth and bush, complete the scene of every old Jamaica township, and the outskirts of the new."—Page 99.

"In villages, and on small settlements, the huts or dwellings of the laborers are composed chiefly of mud walls, sometimes of wattles plastered with the same. * * * In very few cases are they raised off the ground, nor are they floored in any way. * * * Ventilation, or the admission of fresh air, is almost invariably neglected."—Page 100.

"These small, dark, unventilated houses are frequently over-crowded, especially at night; within the small space of a few square feet, perhaps on the bare ground, or may be on a mattress or mat, or in some cases on a bed, with a whole family of eight or nine persons of all ages, and of both sexes, huddled together, with the door and so-called window closed; all clad in the same clothes which they wore through the day, with children sleeping on mattresses often soaked and half rotted with urine and other secretions; should there accidentally be a hole or crevice, this is immediately closed up by means of rags or something of the kind. The rush of odors on opening such a place must be experienced to be understood."—Page 102.

"As regards water for domestic purposes, it is very much to be feared that a large portion of our poor population seldom think of that. Their persons are never abluted save in crossing a river, or being exposed to a heavy shower of rain."—Page 103.

"Among the lower classes, great errors occur in relation to food, both as to quantity, quality, and the period of taking their meals. * * * At night, however, they take what they term their pot; this consists of a sort of soup, composed of salt beef or pork, (if rancid or high, it is preferred), with vegetables of all kinds, highly seasoned, or of salt fish or corned fish, with plantains, yams, cocos, &c.; of this they partake most freely, literally fulfilling the meaning of the expression, 'bellyful.' The meal over, they fall asleep, and as might be expected, are most difficult to arouse."—Page 106.

"In former times, the lower orders of the laboring population were considered to be very abstemious. There appears, however, to be a tendency to excess among many of them, especially those located in towns; their favorite drinks are those compounds known as Anisettes, and liquors of a similar kind."—Page 108.

"Among the lower classes the majority not compelled by circumstances to be field-laborers, are too lazy to move; they frequently squat down all day in a sort of sullen apathy; they eat, and drink, and sleep like the brute that perisheth, but all the more active impulses of their human nature appear to be as little excited as if they were totally wanting."—Page 110.

"It is a well known fact that all the towns and villages contain a large number of persons who have no ostensible means of earning their livelihood; the way in which they subsist is an enigma to themselves and others. Exposure to the night-air is very prevalent among the lower classes; under various excuses they meet in numbers, frequently in the open air, or under temporary sheds, as at the performance of wakes over the dead, and also at their revels of john-canoeing, as it is termed, about Christmas time; on these or other occasions of the kind, they give full scope to animal enjoyment; and at the pitch of the excitement of the prevailing passions their gestures and acts resemble more those of demons than of human beings."—Page 111.

"Among the lower classes of the population there is great reason to fear that little or no advance has been made in the better maxims of social life. If a moral feeling exists among them, it is (not?) shown by the calendars of our criminal courts, where the women complain of rape, or attempt to commit rape, and unhappily they occur incessantly."—Page 112.

"Superstitious habits have always been, and will always be, common in a community like this, composed of individuals of so many different races and countries, many of whom openly profess heathenism. The dark practices of Obeah and Myalism have at times effected a vast amount of mischief in this island."—Page 113.[1]

---

[1] "All the efforts of their pastors to eradicate, by moral and religious instructions, the belief in, and the dread of, this remnant of African barbarism, have failed. *The female natives of Haiti, are adepts in the art.*"—Replies of Dr Chamberlaine. Appendix to Report of Central Board of Health of Jamaica, &c.—Page 158.

"Examine the present sanitary condition of the Island. * * * Observe well the fact that the existing laws, meagre as they are, as relates to sanitary matters, are daily broken, and put to open defiance in our very towns and thoroughfares. * * * Correct all this, and then will immigration prove to us a benefit; then will it be a boon to the liberty-crippled American black, a source of temporal and eternal advantage to the African heathen. Till this is done, any further attempt to induce strangers to embark their fortunes here, can be but to disregard the laws of God and man, and by exposing the deceived to destruction; to bring down greater judgments yet upon the authors of their ruin." —Page 117.

The testimony of Capt. C. B. Hamilton of the royal navy, in 1853, before a committee of the House of Commons, in relation to the condition of that island, is curt and to the point. We present the following extract:

" *Chairman.*—You made use of a phrase some time ago with respect to Jamaica having become a desert. Will you explain to what extent you apply that term?

" *Capt. Hamilton.*—I mean that in going to plantation establishments that had evidently been once splendid buildings, where there had been a great outlay of capital on a grand scale, you find the roofs tumbling in, the places deserted, nobody in them, grass growing in the rooms, and perhaps rats and snakes in those very rooms, and a deserted, melancholy appearance that certainly goes to one's heart to view.

" *Chairman.*—Is that applicable only to one part, or is it the general character ?

" *Capt. Hamilton.*—It is the general character.

" *Mr. Bright.*—That is not the case in Jamaica, but in those particular locations ?

" *Capt. Hamilton.*—No; the general character of Jamaica is, that it gives you the impression of a place going to decay. Speaking of the population of Jamaica, I do not refer to the capitalist planters of old times, but of the present population of Jamaica, and their locations and cultivations.

" *Mr. Bright.*—Do you think the term 'desert' was quite applicable to the state of things there ?

" *Capt. Hamilton.*—I should say peculiarly applicable, without any exaggeration.'"

To this sad picture we will add but one other extract, the crowning testimony of the present desolate

---

[1] Report on the Slave Trade, printed by order of the House of Commons, 1853—page 13.

condition, and social degradation of the population of Jamaica. It is from a speech delivered by the Rev. Dr. King, of Glasgow, Scotland, at a large meeting in Kingston, Jamaica, the very scene of his eloquent and vivid description, where every one of his hearers could have contradicted his statements, had they not been in accordance with the facts. They were not contradicted, but were reported by David Turnbull Esq., one of the British champions of the movement for negro emancipation, and printed in London.

" Allusion has been made to the distressed condition of Jamaica, and I am sure that its distress has not been exaggerated. You inhabit a beautiful island. Its climate is so good, that when its advantages for health shall be better known, I think your colony must come to replace Madeira in British estimation, as a desirable retreat for consumptively disposed patients. Your soil is confessed to be generally excellent. The weeds of your public roads are the ornamental plants of our green-houses and hot-houses. Your very wilds are orchards. The grandeur of your mountains is qualified only by the soft charms of their vegetation, and the bounty of nature has transformed your rocky cliffs into hanging-gardens.

" Your isle has a central position in the ocean, as if
to receive and to dispense the riches of the earth.
You speak one language, and the composition of this
meeting shows that a happy harmony subsists among
the sections of your community. Such facts as these
would lead us to expect prosperity. But instead of
prosperity we witness prostration.

" You have peace, fertility, health—all the usual
guarantees of national well-being—and yet your
leading families are disappearing ; your stately man-
sions are falling into decay; your lovely estates are
thrown up; men's hearts are everywhere failing
them for fear, as if war, or famine, or pestilence
desolated your borders. The existence of such distress is matter of notoriety, but I think it has not
been sufficiently pressed upon public attention,
and especially on British attention, that religion
and education are largely sharing the general
calamity.

" But it is too certain that these highest of all
interests are suffering. On the north side of the
island, and on the south side of the island, numer-
ously attended meetings of missionaries, belonging
to different denominations, have been recently held,
to deliberate on matters of common interest to them,
and all the brethren assembling on these occasions
were agreed in the conviction that the secular and

spiritual instruction of the island are, for the most part, in a low and declining condition.

"They were not less united in assigning the temporal distress of the colony as a principal cause of their peculiar difficulties, and discouragements. While churches and societies at home are diminishing the amount of their assistance to missionary institutions here, the inhabitants are disabled, by their sad reverses, from supporting their own ministers and teachers, as they otherwise might; and persons who have still some means at their disposal, are tempted to plead the badness of the times, as a sufficient apology for restricting their exertions.

"The consequence is, that ministers are returning home; schoolmasters are returning home; and the places of those competent and devoted benefactors are left vacant, or filled by others less qualified to succeed them. To what is this lovely island retrograding? Ye friends of humanity, who have done so much, awake and bestir yourselves, lest all that you have done be undone—lest your work be ruined, and your reward lost! From the scene of the facts, amid a great assembly perfectly qualified to judge the accuracy of my statements, I tell you that the objects on which you have expended so much money, so much labor, so much time, so much life, are in jeopardy; and ignorance, irreligion, superstition, intoxication, profligacy, are hovering, like birds of prey, over your schools and chapels, threatening them with destruction."

Such was the contrast presented to the people of Cuba, between the social condition of the inhabitants of Jamaica and their own, when the new captain-general, the Marquis de Pezuela, arrived at Havana, prepared to carry out the measures which had been pronounced satisfactory by the government of Great Britain. Heedless of the disasters which the enforcement of its vicious and mistaken theories had produced in its own colonies, that government had prosecuted its aims with undiminished energy, as we have shown in our remarks on the political relations of Cuba, and Spain had given a reluctant consent to introduce into the legislation of her colony, measures which had been abhorrent to her, and which endangered not only the connection of Cuba with the crown, but also its social and political existence. A slight effort was made to cover the true tendencies of the new measures, by the manner of their introduction; in the words of Lord Ashton to Señor Fer-

---

[1] "The Jamaica movement for enforcing the slave-trade treaties &c. Prepared at the request of the Kingston Committee. Printed for gratuitous distribution. Charles Gilpin, London, 1852."—Page 70, *et seq.*

rer, the Spanish minister, "it is by 'units' and not by 'cargoes,' that the process of liberation will take place, so that the proceedings will be much less alarming in their general aspect, or in their individual amount."

Previous to the arrival of General Pezuela at Havana, the discussion of the slavery question had been sedulously prevented there, by the government censorship of the press. He entered upon the government of the island on the 3d of December, 1853, and on the 7th and 8th of the same month the "Diario de la Marina," his special organ, contained elaborate articles, in which the former policy of the government was condemned, and the necessity of "progress was urged, and a change insisted upon," although the writer admitted that, "great social phenomena are not suppressed without creating greater embarrassments, or at least equal difficulties with those we aspire to eradicate." The position and new obligations of Spain are thus alluded to in the articles in question :

"A member of the vast community of European nations, and bound to it by a thousand ties of glory and of interest, she could not remain unmoved by the general torrent of thought and idea. With these she has contracted obligations which her honor and her true interest demand she shall comply with."

As these articles were known to emanate directly from the palace, if not from the pen of General Pezuela himself, their publication caused the greatest excitement among the black, and alarm among the white inhabitants. In a few days they were followed by others, in which the intentions of the government were more openly avowed, and the superiority of free labor to slave labor was asserted and defended. The States of Kentucky and Ohio were cited, where, it was stated, " a single glance at the aspect of the streets of Louisville and Cincinnati, reveals the different, and even opposing genius and tendencies of their economical organization,"[1] and the duty of softening the "necessary transition " was admitted.

In the midst of this general excitement a novel decree relating to the " emancipado " negroes was issued,[2] which was soon followed by a new code of laws, establishing a system of free labor,[3] and this was succeeded by another decree relative to the

[1] Diario de la Marina, 18th December, 1853.
[2] General Pezuela's official letter to Count Cañongo, 20th December 1853.
[3] Ordenanza, 23d December, 1853.

" emancipados."[1] The unnecessary ostentation, and exciting language of all of these official documents, greatly increased the alarm of the white inhabitants. Coincident with these measures, the press announced that what the government " had in view is to make a transition from labor that is entirely compulsory, to the organization of labor under a state of complete freedom ;"[2] and the fact is officially acknowledged in General Pezuela's Circular[3] to the local governors and lientenant-governors of the island. A secret consulting circular, which soon became public, was also issued by the government, announcing its intention to permit the introduction of a large number of free negro apprentices from Africa.[4]

The excitement among the black population of Cuba, but more particularly in the capital, caused by these publications, and the accompanying measures of the government, was intense. Numbers of negroes promenaded the streets of the city, taking the wall from the whites, for the avowed purpose of exhibiting their sense of their expected new civil rights; while others, more bold, sought the promenades and places of public resort, where they asser-

[1] Ordenanza, 1st January, 1854.
[2] Diario de la Marina, 26th December, 1853.
[3] Gobierno y Capitania General Circular, 23d December, 1853.
[4] Marquis de Pezuela, Circular, 18th January, 1854.

ted their equality of social position, by saluting the ladies, and paying them compliments in impudent and audible commendations of their beauty. The insolence of the slaves carried alarm into the bosom of every family, and the public consequences were in consonance with the predictions which the Count de Villanueva, and the ayuntamiento of Havana had so truthfully and boldly laid before General Espartero, when regent of Spain, in 1841.

Men prepared for revolution as the only means of self-preservation. Cubans and Spaniards united cordially in this determination, and preparations were made almost openly for the coming event. Some intimation of the occurrences probably came to the knowledge of General Pezuela, for a remonstrance against the new policy, signed by a large number of the most prominent citizens of Havana, was sent to Spain. At the same time he could not be ignorant of the excitement in the public mind, and he endeavored to allay it, by proclamation,[1] continuing at the same time to carry out the previously prepared measures. The decree of 3d May, 1854, directing the registry of the slaves, preparatory "to measures of a more transcendent nature, the approval of which, by her majesty, the queen," was expected, was introduced by a public address,

---

[1] Proclamation, 3d May, 1854.

denying the existence of any treaty with a foreign nation, "the basis of which is the emancipation of the slaves," and styling the rumors then agitating the public mind, "a chattering and shameful war of letters and lies." The same public address contained the remarkable announcement, that while the government would fulfill its duty, "the inhabitants of Cuba have another duty, not less sacred, to attend to—complying with the laws; it is time for it to make the life of the creole negro more sweet than that of the white, who, under another name, labors to exhaustion in Europe."

This proclamation and decree only tended to increase and confirm the public alarm, and it was further augmented by a knowledge of the succeeding measures of the government. On the 22nd of May, General Pezuela directed the Bishop of Havana to suspend the law of the Church interdicting the marriage of whites with blacks, which was accordingly done by a circular to the officiating priests, dated 29th of that month.[1] At the same time a militia of free blacks and mulattoes was directed to be organized[2] throughout the island, which was put upon an equal footing, with regard to privilege, with the regular army.

[1] Secretaria del Obispado de la Habana, Circular No. 50.

[2] Ordenanza, 24th May, 1854.

In conjunction with these measures, the white inhabitants were disarmed, the officers of the government collecting all the arms in possession of private citizens. The popular ferment which followed these measures alarmed General Pezuela, and on the 30th May, he issued his celebrated retracting proclamation, announcing that the government would not interfere with the social institutions of the country, for "that unhappy race which comprehends freedom to be vagrancy, * * * once placed among civilized men, protected by religion, and by the great laws of our fathers, is, in its so-called slavery, a thousand times more happy than other classes in Europe, which have freedom only in name." The press, too, was silenced, and although General Pezuela ceased from that time to initiate the new policy, the public alarm did not subside. The home government, fearing to lose its colony, at a time when its allies were too much engrossed by the difficulties of the war in the East to assist it, removed him, and confided to General Concha, for the second time, the government of Cuba.

The critical circumstances of the colony at this period, induced the court to grant more extraordinary powers to the new captain-general, than had been held by any of his predecessors. The heads of the Treasury and Marine departments, which were for-

merly co-equal with, are now subject to the captain-
general; and the authority of all the local organizations has been greatly reduced, so that the governor
of Cuba now holds the most completely centralized
and irresponsible power in the New World.

General Concha's first care was to endeavor to
calm the public mind, and to reassure it of the
safety of the existing social institutions. In this he
in a great measure succeeded; but as none of the
measures instituted by General Pezuela have been
rescinded; as the black and mulatto troops have not
been disarmed, but have been made a permanent
corps of the Spanish army;[1] and as no arms have
been returned, or allowed to the white inhabitants,
a jealous feeling of insecurity pervades the minds of
all reflecting men in Cuba; and the general impression is, that the new policy has only been delayed
to be renewed at a more opportune moment. Before
contemplating the possible future of the social question in Cuba, we will present a few considerations
upon the composition of the two unmixed races.

The black population of Cuba is composed of the
negroes born in the island, and a large number
which have been imported from the Gold coast, the
country around the mouth of the Congo river, and

General Order, 7th August, 1855.

4

from Mozambique. It is difficult to ascertain its exact numbers, as is shown in the chapter on population in the following work, and there is great diversity in the estimates of different statisticians. Those who regard the smaller number as most reliable, besides committing the error of adopting the statistics of sugar planting for general application to the country, place great reliance upon the disparity in number of the sexes, and from this they assume a necessary decrease of numbers in the total population. In our reflections upon this disparity of the sexes, we have observed two facts which we have never seen presented in any argument upon the question, and which we think have had an important relation to the law of population in Cuba.

The disparity between the sexes has arisen from the nature of the African slave-trade, which has always brought a larger number of males than females; the proportions being, so far as our limited means of information enable us to judge, somewhere between 4 to 1 and 5 to 1. Yet, notwithstanding this disparity of the sexes arriving in Cuba, the proportion of males to females among the negroes there, in 1825, is set down by the accurate Humboldt, as 1 to 1.7; and he recognizes the fact that an improvement in this regard was going on. In fact, among the negroes born in the island no disparity of the sexes is found; this must, therefore, be sought among the imported slaves, and its effect upon their numbers ascertained.

The proportion of females imported by the slave traders is, as we have stated somewhere, between 1 to 4 and 1 to 5. We believe we may safely assume the ratio of 175 per 1,000 of all, an equal number being also boys between ten and fourteen years of age. The females imported by the slave traders are, for obvious reasons, very nearly, or quite all, women of the productive age, who have never borne children. This proportion of productive women is very large, as will be seen by the statistics of this country. Dr. Jarvis, in his letters to the Census Office, says, "The females in Massachusetts, between twenty and forty, in 1840, were 163 per 1,000 of all, and in the United States 143 per 1,000." By the census of 1850 the proportion of white females between the same ages was 148 per 1,000 of all; and the proportion of those between twenty and thirty, which would approximate more nearly to, though still be far from, equalling the class of females imported among the slaves in Cuba, is only 81 per 1,000 of all. It should also be remembered, in seeking for the law of population in Cuba, that the female

[1] Compendium of United States Census, p. 122, *note.*

slaves imported there are under more favorable conditions for reproduction, than even those between twenty and thirty, in the United States, from the fact that, though they are of the productive age, a very small portion of them have ever borne children.

These facts lead us to believe that the conclusions applicable to population in other countries, should be modified in Cuba; and that in their effects may be found, the explanations of the seeming contradictions between the supposed necessary decrease of the slave population, and the position and rapid advance of the island in population and material prosperity. The number of slaves in Cuba we estimate, as will be seen in the chapter on population in the following work, at about six hundred and sixty thousand. Their character in general is that of a very docile and obedient class, and the distinctions of their several native tribes are kept up of their own accord. To this number we have to add about two hundred and twenty thousand free blacks and mulattoes; making a total of eight hundred and eighty thousand Africans and their descendants.

The white, or European race, as we have termed it, numbers nearly five hundred and sixty-five thousand. The official tables of 1846 give the following as the numbers of the foreign born white population. Natives of Spain, 27,264 (exclusive of the army, to which no Cubans are admitted); Canary Islands, 19,759; other Antilles, 1,361; United States, 1,256; other parts of America, 2,334; France, 2,066; Great Britain, 605; other countries, 842.

The Spaniards are very nearly all office-holders and traders, it being seldom that they purchase land or real estate. Wielding thus the power and ready capital of the country, their political influence is great, while their impress upon the social character of the community is very limited. The natives of the Canary Islands are largely engaged in the minor branches of agriculture, and assimilate readily with the native whites. Many of the French are planters; of the English, a large number are connected with the mining interests. The great majority of the American citizens in Cuba are machinists and mechanics, in which class are also found large numbers of French and British subjects. To this fact we trace the great contrast observed in the state of the mechanic arts in Cuba and in the mother country, and the much greater advance of the former in the adoption of mechanical appliances to labor. The machinists, carpenters, coopers, masons, carriage-makers, smiths, &c., of Cuba, being mostly Americans and French, or such as have learned the trades in their shops, the manner of labor, tools, and style of work in Cuba, resemble ours much more than they do those of Spain, or of Spanish America, and have given to her civilization a resemblance to that of the Anglo-American, not found elsewhere out of the United States.

This resemblance has been increased by the proximity and frequency of intercourse between the two countries, by an identity of t.cial institutions and aspirations, and by the large number of Cuban youth educated here. It is estimated that for many years very nearly two thousand boys from Cuba have been pursuing their studies in American schools. The ideas and manner of thought with which they return to the island, are more American than Spanish, and these are continually extended by their influence and their example.

Such is the social condition of Cuba, and the influences which bear upon it. In conclusion, we will present a few considerations upon its possible future. We have seen that Spain has declared that when the island ceases to be Spanish, it shall become African, and that there is good reason to believe that in view of the impossibility of holding it many years longer, she has acceded to the solicitations of other European powers, and consented to bring it under the rule of the social theories now prevailing in all the other European colonies in the Antilles. We have seen that the people of Cuba now stand alone in their resistance to this social revolution and ruin. The advance of the emancipation theories of Europe in the Antilles, and the gradual extinction of the white race there, is unmistakably indicated by the state of the British West Indies. There we see at a glance the true tendencies and results of the application of the social theories of Europe to the communities of America. The details of their history show the sufferings of the whites, and the decline of public prosperity and social welfare; and indicate an ultimate state of barbarism as the social condition of the West India Islands. These truths are acknowledged by very. competent authority in Great Britain. One of the leading London journals lately held the following language on this subject.[1]

"We have of late, as occasion served, directed the attention of our readers to the condition of the most valuable of our West India possessions, and have endeavored to trace to its true source, in a vicious and mistaken policy, the ruin which not only impends, but has actually fallen upon those islands, once the boast and glory of the British Crown—now the by-word of the commercial nations of the earth. Jamaica, by nature the richest of these dependencies, is reduced to a state of collapse, from which recovery

[1] London Morning Herald, 8th September, 1855. ι

seems to be hopeless. Efforts have been made to stimulate once more her industry, to raise her crushed proprietary, and to give them once again opportunity and hope. So far those efforts have not been successful. In the recent advices we can perceive no symptoms of amendment; on the contrary, the downward tendency of affairs continues, as if for the unhappy Jamaicans there is a "lower deep" yet yawning, which "threatening, opens to devour," and from whose frightful vortex there seems to be no hope of escape."

* * * * * *

" Although the ruin of Jamaica has been more rapid and irresistible than any of the other islands, desolation rests upon the entire Archipelago, and sooner or later will involve them all."

This present desolation of the British Antilles is the dark future which the inhabitants of Cuba are called upon to avert from themselves, and from their children, and which has impelled them to declare to the Spanish government, that the attempt to introduce there the social theories of European philanthropy must produce a bloody revolution, for no white man will be disposed to submit to so hard a fate. This revolution may soon degenerate to a war of races in Cuba, as Spain has declared her reliance upon the blacks, and other European powers have instigated and sustained her in this declaration. Such a war would arouse the sympathies of the people of the United States in favor of the whites in Cuba, to a pitch of popular excitement that has never been witnessed, and no laws of neutrality or considerations of policy, could prevent their immediate and direct interference and assistance. The result would be the utter annihilation of the black race in Cuba, which might lead to a war of extermination against them in all the larger Antilles. Who can contemplate such a result without shuddering? What philanthropy can advocate a policy which must attain such terrible results!

No public indications at present exist of a disposition on the part of the powers of western Europe, to abandon their attempts to extend over Cuba, the theories which have ruined Jamaica and her sister colonies. Rather do they urge Spain to establish them as the surest means of preventing the advance of the American confederacy in that direction. Thus is the social ruin of a neighboring island, one of the contingents in the conflict between the American and European policies, between republicanism and monarchism; and in the natural course of events Cuba may yet become the Crimea, and Havana the Sebastopol, of the New World.

4*

The European manner of mis-stating that complex combination of questions of American international and civil policy, generally known as the Cuban Question, is thus adroitly and characteristically practised, by one of the British reviews, most zealously liberal, after the manner of European liberalism.

" If then the slave States do gain Cuba, they may possibly gain a loss. If they conquer her they will find her emancipated or desolated; if they purchase her they will buy a colored population more insubordinate than any they have now; and even if these dangers do not realize themselves, an economical result, as Mr. Robertson well explains,[1] may follow, by which the abolitionists may, after all, be the real gainers. Were Cuba once peacefully possessed by enterprising Americans, the cultivation of her soil, and with it the demand for slaves, would be greatly increased, while one great source of supply, the African slave-trade, would be stopped. At the same time the insular population would decrease rather than increase, by reason of the disparity of the sexes; the sole resource, therefore, would be the slave-breeding States of Virginia, North Carolina, and Maryland; and the inducement to them to sell

[1] " A Few Months in America, by James Robertson." London, 1855.

would probably be so great as to draw away their stock, until they became free States—a far greater gain to the North than Cuba would be to the South. Meantime, however, the slave party still desires annexation; it disregards or despises its dangers, or rather it loses sight of them in fear of what may happen, if it does not annex. Here we have the true meaning of the Lone Star Lodges and Ostend Conferences. The Americans try to make the Cuban whites imitate them in casting off their allegiance to the mother country, because they fear that Spain will imitate us in compelling emancipation."— *Westminster Review*, July, 1855. Reprint, p. 97.

This is an adroit and characteristic mis-statement of the Cuban question. Its opening assumption that the northern and southern States of the American Union are opposed to each other in their vital interests, is the artful insinuation of the defenders of European policy, in their opposition to American theories, but it is an error of fact. However great may be the sectional jealousies and irritation, at the present time or in the past (for when have they ceased to exist?), the vital interests of the North and the South are the same. The integrity of the territory of the North, is the integrity of the territory of the South, and when the question of the northeastern

boundary threatened a hostile invasion of the State
of Maine, at a time when the waves of sectional
feeling ran fierce and high, the South was as ready
and as ardent in the determination to defend the
national honor, and the national domain, as any
other portion of the Union. So too, should any
attempt be made upon the integrity of the territory
of the South, or of the Pacific States, through our
defenceless condition in the mid-American waters,
and the Pacific Ocean, no one doubts that the great
heart of the North would respond at once, and
with enthusiasm, to the call of our common
country.

The same intimate sympathy between the North
and the South exists in their material interests. Do
the seasons prove unpropitious, and the crops of the
South fail; the North feels the common loss in every
pulsation of her commercial and fabrile industry.
Do the grains and meats of the North and West,
cease to come forward with their accustomed plenty;
or do the ships of the East lie idly at the wharves;
the South experiences the consequent languor in
every nerve. The glorious memories of our land,
too, are linked in sympathetic union; Lexington and
Bunker Hill, Saratoga and Monmouth, Yorktown
and Fort Moultrie, New Orleans and Plattsburg, are
names equally dear to the North and to the South;

while the glorious achievements of our common
arms in Mexico, show only the most fraternal rivalry
to enhance the common glory. The confederacy is,
in fact, one mighty whole, and whoever will contemplate it apart from the mists of local politics, will
not fail to be impressed with this truth.

The question of the accession of Cuba to the confederacy is not a local question, but stands upon this
broad national ground. It is pertinent not only to
the South, but to the East, North, and West. Is it
a question of national defence? Cuba guards all the
approaches south of Charleston to our eastern national frontier. Is it a question of the safety of our
domestic intercourse? Cuba guarantees the safety of
the routes of commerce between the Ocean and the
Gulf of Mexico, and between the Atlantic and Pacific States. The commercial and industrial relations
of Cuba to the United States, are also as national as
is her geographical position. The lumbermen, the
fisheries, and the shipping of New England, have a
deep present interest in her welfare, while the wants
of her people offer a great natural outlet to the manufacturing industry of the same States, which is now
closed to them by artificial barriers.

The miners, machinists, farmers, merchants, and
manufacturers of the Middle States, carry on, even
now, vast exchanges with her productive industry.

The rice and lumber of the South find their greatest
and best foreign market in Cuba. The grain and
meats of the West, now in a great measure shut out
from Cuba by the restrictions of a jealous tariff,
would find in her accession to the confederacy, a
market to the value of millions annually from the
store of their ever-increasing plenty. Is it a question of civil or of international policy ? The extension of our theories of government to Cuba must
contribute to their stability, strengthen the ties of
our civil policy, increase its moral power, and augment our weight in the family of nations. The
accession of Cuba to the Union is not, therefore,
merely a Southern question, but it is a question of
national gain and of national power.

The assertion, that " if they conquer her they will
find her emancipated or desolated," is the reiteration
of the. barbarous and savage threat of Spain—that
"Cuba shall ever remain Spanish or become African."
The heart that can conceive, and the liberalism that
can reiterate, such a threat, are only worthy of the
highest reprobation. But it involves an error of
fact, in assuming that a disposition exists on the part
of the United States to conquer Cuba. Such an idea
has never been broached in this country, nor do we
believe it has ever been entertained by any one.
The truth is, that American sympathizers have been

willing to aid the people of Cuba in an effort to conquer the Spanish power there.

European writers, in contemplating the accession of new countries to the American confederation, studiously forget, or avoid the fact, that it is not some powerful king, surrounded by courtiers and privileged classes of nobility, extending his sway over new conquests and subjugated nations; but it is the extension of the right of self-government by the people, and their integrity in the great arena of freedom, guaranteed by the jealous watchfulness of the whole. Should the people of Cuba successfully assert their rights, and seek admission to the American confederacy, there would be no conquest but that of right over might, and of freedom over oppression.

That "they may find her emancipated or desolated," that is to say, African, or a heap of mouldering ashes, is apparently a bold threat; but to our view it is only the ebullition of fear and weakness. We know that neither the liberalism nor the governments of Europe have ever recognized the existence of the people of Cuba as a body politic; but this in no wise affects its vitality, nor the influence which a successful assertion of its rights may have upon itself, or upon its relations to other powers. A people numbering almost six hundred thousand free and intelligent whites; inhabiting a country whose area is very nearly equal to that of England proper; the productions of whose industry rule many of the most important markets of the world; whose geographical position is one of the most marked upon the globe; and the ratio of whose industrial and social progress is exceeded by only one among existing nations, does not depend, for its being, upon its recognition in European reviews, or in cautiously-written, and guardedly-worded, diplomatic notes. The people of Cuba, by their labor, and the fertility of her soil, have already stamped the fact of their existence in unmistakable characters upon the industrial world, and in the struggle for their rights, and for their very existence, which any attempt to carry out the barbarous threat thus held forth by Spaniards, and by Englishmen, would surely create, the assertion of their rights would have a like effect upon their political relations with other nations.

That if Spain relinquished her forcibly-maintained sovereignty over Cuba, by sale or treaty, to the United States, the confederacy would "buy a colored population more insubordinate than any they now have," is an assertion in regard to the future, which we do not deem justified by the general principles which regulate cause and effect.

In what manner the transfer of a sovereignty from

Spain to a free people, in which the Cubans would be included, would produce such a complete and radical change in the disposition of her servile class, we are not informed, and we cannot conceive. The relation between master and slave is the same in Cuba and in the United States; and if the European writer draws his conclusion from a supposed savage disposition on the part of the native Africans, now in Cuba, we think he judges them without a personal knowledge of their character, that he forgets two essential points; that they were not warriors, but mere slaves in Africa, and have never known any other condition; and that they never have been exposed, by community of language, and facility of access, to the bloodthirsty teachings of European philanthropy.

The economical anticipations of Mr. Robertson and the reviewer may, or may not be realized; but we can have no great confidence in the anticipations of the political economy of the European philanthropists, while we contemplate the disastrous results which have attended the experiment of their social theories in the British West Indies. On this point we would suggest to them a consideration of the wise observations of Baron Humboldt, addressed to those who anticipated direful results from the cessation of the slave-trade:

"The prognostications which some too lightly make * * * do not seem to me sufficiently conclusive. They do not take into consideration the fact * * * that the increase of the total population of Cuba, when the importation of negroes from Africa shall have ceased entirely, is based upon elements so complicated, upon such various *compensations* of effect upon the white, free colored, and slave population * * * that we should not anticipate such mournful presages, but wait until positive statistical data have been obtained."

That "the Americans try to make the Cuban whites imitate them in casting off their allegiance to the mother country, because they fear that Spain will imitate us in compelling emancipation," is one of those mis-statements characteristic of European writers upon American questions. The desire of the people of Cuba for liberation from European thraldom, is purely and entirely of Cuban origin. It was the natural desire of a people for that freedom which they contemplated in the countries around them, and existed long before they turned their hopes to this country for assistance. The conspiracies that, from 1822 to 1828, threatened the existence of the Spanish power in Cuba, were the spontaneous growth of public feeling, as were those of 1835, under Gen.

Lorenzo, in St. Jago; and of Gen. Lopez, in 1848, in Cienfuegos. The flight of Gen. Lopez and others to the United States, upon the premature discovery of their plans, first induced the patriots of Cuba to look to the people of this country for assistance; and the fact that they have found sympathy and aid here, is the natural result of a community of political aspirations and interests, and of the great American necessity of resistance to the open and covert assaults of European policy, upon our institutions and their influence.

We have alluded to this stereotyped European statement, and argument of the Cuban question, because we consider it aimed, not at the simple question whether Cuba shall remain Spanish or not, but against the extension over new territories of those principles of government, which are so successfully maintained here, and of our political theories, which are viewed with so much dislike by the advocates and defenders of European kingcraft. We deem the question of the future social condition and political relations of Cuba, as not only of pressing and vital importance to herself, but as intimately connected with the peace and progress of our own confederacy, and through that with the ultimate success of the republican theory of government.

The idea that Cuba will some day belong to the

United States, exists solely from a contemplation of moral possibilities, and not from any admission of the fact by the European mind; and the statesmen of Europe are laboring strenuously to prevent its accomplishment. The policy of the British cabinet on this point is strikingly exhibited in Lord Palmerston's assertion, that "if the negro population of Cuba were rendered free, that fact would create a most powerful element of resistance to any scheme for annexing Cuba to the United States." In this he is undoubtedly right. Emancipation in Cuba would blot that country, and its productions, now so important in the commerce of all civilized nations, from the list of wealth-producing communities. It would call into existence, in immediate proximity to our southern shores, a negro community, under the influence of the European idea and policy, which would be dangerous to us as a neighbor, and worse than dangerous to us as a part of this confederacy; or, perhaps, worse still, it might initiate a war of races in Cuba, from a participation in which no power or considerations could prevent our people, and which might prove alike disastrous to the blacks in the Antilles, and to our own domestic repose.

In this question England is arrayed in hostility against us, for the questions of Emancipation and Slavery are the Scylla and Charybdis of our confederacy, and if the class government that rules Great Britain can make it a deadly hostility to us, they are forced to do so by the very exigencies of self-preservation. The statesmen of England know, and so do those of America, that the race for life is now being run by the broad and genial republican theories of America, and the limited and partial theories of that simulacro of freedom—European constitutional monarchy. One or the other of these systems must perish. If republicanism triumphs, England must concede the five points to her people, and seek her defence against the autocratic theories of Europe, in a sincere friendship with America. If constitutional monarchy triumphs, and this Union is dismembered, the theory of a democratic representative government will have failed before the world, and the effete theories of Europe will pass safely through the crisis that now attends them, and receive new vigor from the scattered elements that now constitute our vitality and moral power.

It is because the aristocratic classes that govern England are well aware of these truths, and see in them the ultimate extinction of their class-system of goverfiment, that Great Britain has never yet taken the stand of true friendship to this country. When impelled by interest, for a feeling of popular sympathy has never impelled her to it, they have

acquiesced in a present seeming friendship. But
the retention of the frontier forts after the revolution; the intrigues in Europe against our early commercial treaties; the orders in council; the war of
1812; the treaty of Ghent, and the fishery question
at that time; the northeastern boundary; the Ore-
gon question; the efforts against our acquisition of
Texas; the intrigues in the war and treaty with
Mexico; the South Carolina correspondence; the
intrigues in Nicaragua and Dominica against us;
the questions of free trade with Canada, and of the
rights of our fishermen, afford demonstrations as
clear as any in Euclid of the animus that moves them.

The Cuban question is the same disease in its
most aggravated and worst form. While Spain, under the instigation of England, and supported by
that power and France, is giving life and energy to
her hatred and their hostility to us, in the policy she
has adopted in Cuba, the British cabinet may well
put on the mask of friendship, and assure us, as she
has already done on one occasion, that all will be
right with her fond ally Spain. And when the evil
is done, when the work of hate is consummated,
when Cuba has perished before the sirocco breath of
European philanthropy, and the seeds of dissension
and disunion are sown broadcast through the length
and breadth of this great confederacy, then may

England's statesmen weep crocodile tears over our misfortunes, and be sad, in mockery, at our fate. The truth is, that England and France have not a tithe of the fear of a war between this country and Spain, that they have of the extension of our political theories over Cuba, and the triumph of the American theory—that States having different social organizations, can exist and prosper in political union; and of the consequent consolidation of American power on this continent, and of its influence throughout the world.

HUMBOLDT'S CUBA.

CHAPTER I

GENERAL VIEWS.

Political importance of the island of Cuba and port of Havana
—Their relations to contiguous countries—Increase of public
wealth and revenue—Description of Bay and City of Havana—
Public buildings—Streets—Public walks and grounds—Ashes
of Columbus—Palms—Vicinity of Havana—Suburbs—Projected
moat—Defences of Havana—Population—Increase—Marriages,
births, and deaths—Hospitals—Health—Markets—Hospitality—
[NOTE.—Establishment of Navy yard at Havana—Don Augustin
de Arriola—List of ships built at Havana—Abandonment of the
Navy-yard.]

THE political importance of the island of Cuba
does not arise solely from its great extent, though it
is one half larger than Haiti, nor from the admirable
fertility of its soil, nor from its great naval resources,[1]
nor from the nature of its population, three-fourths
of which are freemen; but it derives a far greater

[1] See Note at the end of the chapter.

political influence through the advantages which result from the geographical position of the city and harbor of Havana.

That northern portion of the sea of the Antilles known as the Gulf of Mexico, forms a circular bay of more than two hundred and fifty leagues diameter, as it were, a Mediterranean with two outlets, whose coasts from Cape Florida to Cape Catoche, in Yucatan, appertain exclusively, at the present time, to the confederations of the Mexican States and of North America. The island of Cuba, or more properly speaking, that part of its shore between Cape San Antonio and the city of Matanzas, situate near the entrance of the old Bahama channel, closes the Gulf of Mexico on the southeast, leaving to the oceanic current we call the Gulf Stream, no other passages than a strait on the south, between Cape San Antonio and Cape Catoche, and the Bahama channel on the north, between Bahia Honda and the reefs of Florida.

Near to the northern outlet, and immediately where a multitude of highways thronging with the commerce of the world cross each other, lies the beautiful port of Havana, strongly defended by nature, and still more strongly fortified by art. Fleets sailing from this port, built in part of the cedar and mahogany of Cuba, may defend the passages to the American Mediterranean and menace the opposite coasts, as the fleets sailing from Cadiz may hold the dominion of the ocean near the Columns of Hercules. The Gulf of Mexico, and the old and new Bahama channels unite under the meridian of Havana. The opposing flow of their currents, and the violent atmospherical agitations natural there, particularly at the beginning of winter, give a peculiar character to this spot on the northern boundary of the equinoctial zone.

The island of Cuba is not only the largest of the Antilles (being nearly equal to England proper without the principality of Wales), but from its long and narrow form, its great extent of coast makes it at once contiguous with Haiti, Jamaica, Florida (the southern State of the United States), and Yucatan, the eastern State of Mexico. This circumstance is worthy of the most mature consideration, for these countries (Cuba, Jamaica, Haiti, and the southern portions of the United States, from Louisiana to Virginia), distant but a few days' sail from each other, contain nearly two millions eight hundred thousand Africans. As St. Domingo, Florida, and Mexico have been separated from Spain, Cuba does not assimilate politically with the countries it borders, although as they were for many ages subject to the same laws, it has a similarity of religion, language, and customs.

Florida forms the most southern link of that great chain of republics whose northern boundary touches the upper waters of the river St. Lawrence, and which extends from the region of palms to that of the most rigorous winter. The inhabitants of New England believe that the progressive increase of the blacks, the preponderance of the States they inhabit, (the slave States,) and a preference for the culture of the colonial staples, are public dangers. Therefore, they do not wish to cross the Straits of Florida, the present boundary of the great American confederacy, except for the purposes of a free commerce based upon an equality of rights. It is true they fear any event which may throw Cuba into the hands of a more formidable European power than Spain, but undoubtedly they desire no less strongly that the ties which formerly bound Cuba to Louisiana, Pensacola, and St. Augustine, shall remain for ever broken.

The vicinity of Florida has never been of much importance to the trade of Havana, from the sterility of her soil and her want of inhabitants and cultivation. But this is not the case with respect to the coasts of Mexico, which, extending in a semi-circle from the more frequented ports of Tampico, Vera Cruz, and Alvarado to Cape Catoche, almost join through the peninsular of Yucatan to the western portion of Cuba. The illicit trade between Havana and the port of Campeachy is not only very active, but is increasing, notwithstanding the efforts of the new government of Mexico against it; for of the many vessels engaged in the contraband traffic with Havana, but a small number are engaged in the traffic with the more distant coasts of Caraccas and Colombia. The necessary supplies of salted meats (jerked beef), for the slaves in Cuba, are procured from Buenos Ayres and the plains of Merida more easily, and with less danger in these unquiet times, than from Cumaná, New Barcelona, or Caraccas.

It is well known that Cuba and the Archipelago of the Philippine Islands have for centuries drawn from the treasury of Mexico the sums necessary for their internal administration, and for the preservation of their fortifications, their arsenals and their navy yards. Havana has been the naval port of Mexico, as I have stated in another work,[1] and received annually (until 1808) from its treasury more than one million eight hundred thousand dollars.

[1] "In the present state of affairs, (1803–4), the coast of Mexico is a military dependence of Havana, which is the only neighboring port that affords shelter to squadrons; it is therefore the most important point in the defence of the eastern shores of Mexico. For this reason the government has expended enormous sums in its fortification since its capture by the English. The court of Madrid, fully aware of its own interests, has established the principle that in order to preserve Mexico, the dominion of the island of Cuba must be maintained."—*Humboldt.* "*Political Essay on New Spain.*"

Even in Madrid, for a long time, Cuba and the Philipine Islands were considered as dependencies of Mexico, situat d at distances widely apart, east and west from the ports of Vera Cruz and Acapulco, but united to the Mexican metropolis, which was then a European colony, by all the ties of commerce, of mutual assistance, and of ancient affection.

The increase of her own proper wealth has gradually made this assistance from the Mexican treasury unnecessary to Cuba. Of all the Spanish possessions she has been the most prosperous, and the port of Havana has risen, since the disasters of St. Domingo, to the rank of a first-class mart in the commercial world. A happy concurrence of political circumstances, the moderation of the government officials, and the conduct of the inhabitants, who are keen, prudent, and careful of their own interests, have preserved to Havana the continued enjoyment of a free interchange with foreign nations. The revenue from her customs has increased so greatly, that Cuba not only covers her own expenditures, but during the war between Spain and her continental colonies, has contributed large sums to relieve the remnants of the army from Venezuela, for the defence of the castle of San Juan de Ulua, and to the costly and most generally fruitless naval armaments that Spain has fitted out.

I have been twice in Cuba, on one occasion three months, and on the other a month and a half, and have had the good fortune to enjoy the confidence of persons, who from their talents and position, either as proprietors, administrators, or merchants, could give me reliable information regarding the advance of public prosperity. This confidence flowed from the favor with which I was honored by the Spanish ministry, and I trust that I also merited it for the moderation of my principles, my circumspect conduct, and for the pacific character of my occupation. For the last thirty years the Spanish government has not obstructed the publication, even in Havana, of the most interesting statistical tables relative to the state of the commerce, colonial agriculture, and revenue of Cuba. I obtained copies of these documents during my stay there, and the relations I have preserved with America since my return to Europe, have afforded me the complement of the data I had previously collected.

I visited in company with Bonpland only the vicinity of Havana, the beautiful valley of Güines, and the coast between Batabanó and Trinidad. After describing succinctly the physical aspect of the country, and the singular modifications of a climate so different from that of the other Antilles, I shall speak of the general population of the island, its area calculated from the most exact delineation of its shores, its staples of product and commerce, and the condition of its public revenues.

The view of Havana from the entrance to the port is one of the most picturesque and pleasing on the northern equinoctial shores of America. This view, so justly celebrated by travellers of all nations, does not possess the luxury of vegetation that adorned the banks of the Guayaquil, nor the wild majesty of the rocky coasts of Rio Janeiro, two ports in the southern hemisphere; but the beauty that in our climate adorns the scenes of cultivated nature, unites here with the majesty of the vegetable creation, and with the organic vigor that characterizes the torrid zone. The European who experiences this union of pleasing impressions, forgets the danger that menaces him in the midst of the populous cities of the Antilles, and strives to comprehend the different elements of so vast a country, gazing upon the fortresses crowning the rocks east of the port, the opening arm of the sea surrounded with villages and farmhouses, the tall palms, and the city itself half hidden by a forest of spars and sails of shipping.

The entrance to the harbor of Havana passes between the Morro Castle (*castillo de los Santos Reyes*) and the fort of *San Salvador de la Punta*; its width is from 360 to 450 yards which it preserves for three-fifths of a mile, when, leaving on the north the Castle of *San Carlos de la Cabaña*, and the village of Casa Blanca, it opens into a large trefoil shaped bay, the greatest width of which, from N. N. E. to S. S. W. is two miles and a half. The three smaller bays which open from it are called Guanabacoa, Guasabacoa, and Atares, the latter containing several springs of fresh water.

The city of Havana, surrounded by walls, is built upon a promontory, extending from the Navy-yard on the south, to the Punta fort on the north. In the harbor, beyond the remains of some vessels that have been sunk and the little isle of Luz, there are only eight or ten, or, perhaps, more correctly speaking, five or six fathoms of water. The castles Atares and San Carlos del Principe defend the city on the western side inland, one of them being 1,400 and the other 2,630 yards from the wall of the city. The intermediate space comprises the suburbs of Horcon, Jesus Maria, and Salud, which encroach yearly upon the Campo Marte.

The principal edifices of Havana, the Cathedral, the Government House, the residence of the Comandante of Marine, the Navy-yard, the Post-office, and the Royal Tobacco factory, are less notable for their beauty than for the solidity of their construction. The streets are generally narrow, and many of them not paved. As the paving stone is brought from Vera Cruz, and its transportation is costly, the singular idea had been entertained, shortly before my arrival, of supplying its place with great trunks of trees, as is done in Germany and Russia, in the construction of dikes across swampy places. This project was speedily abandoned; but travellers who arrived subsequently to the making of the experiment, were surprised to see beautiful trunks of mahogany buried in the ruts of Havana.

During my residence in Spanish America few of the cities presented a more disgusting appearance than did Havana, from the want of a good police. One walked through the mud to the knees, and the many carriages, or *volantes*, which are the characteristic carriages of this city, and the drays laden with boxes of sugar, their drivers rudely elbowing the passer-by, made walking in the streets both vexatious and humiliating.[1] The offensive odor of the salted meat, or *tasajo*, infected many of the houses, and even some of the ill-ventilated streets. It is said the police have remedied these evils, and that

---

[1] These evils have since that time been in a very great measure remedied, and Havana is now as well paved, and lighted with gas as the best regulated city of America or Europe, while a better police system has removed many of the inconveniences of walking in the streets.

lately there has been a marked improvement in the cleanliness of the streets. The houses are well ventilated, and the street *de los Mercaderes* presents a beautiful view. There, as in many of our older cities in Europe, the adoption of a bad plan when laying out the city can only be slowly remedied.

There are two good promenades; one, the Alameda, inside the walls, between the theatre and the hospice of Paula; and the other outside the walls, running from the Punta fort to the Muralla gate. The first was ornamented with much taste by Peruani, an Italian artist, in 1803; and the second, known as the extra-mural *paseo*, is a delightfully cool resort, and generally after sunset is filled with carriages. Its construction was commenced by the Marquis de la Torre, who, of all the governors sent to Cuba, was the first to give an impulse to the improvement of the police and the municipal regimen of Havana. Don Luis de las Casas, whose memory is also held in high esteem by the inhabitants of Havana, and the Count de Santa Clara, have both improved these grounds.[1]

The botanical garden, near *Campo Marte*, is w...

[1] A third beautiful *paseo*, with gardens, was added to these in 1836, by General Tacon; and subsequent governors have improved the old roads and opened several new ones around Havana; so that its vicinity now affords many delightful drives.

thy of the attention of the government. Since my
return to Europe a marble statue of Carlos III. has
been erected in the extra-mural *paseo*. Its site had
been first selected for a monument to Columbus,
whose ashes were brought to Havana on the cession
of the Spanish part of St. Domingo to the French.
The remains of Hernan Cortés having been carried
during the same year (1796) from one church in
Mexico to another, there occurred the coincidence
of a re-interment at the same time, near the close of
the eighteenth century, of the two greatest of the
men who were made illustrious by the discovery
and conquest of America.[1]

[1] " The line-of-battle ship, San Lorenzo, arrived at Havana on the
15th January, 1796, bearing, in a rich coffin, the venerated ashes of
Columbus. . Generals Las Casas and Araoz and bishops Trespalacios
and Peñalver received them on the shore, amid the entire garrison
formed for the occasion, and deposited them with solemn ceremo-
nials in their resting-place in the cathedral, in that humble niche
where they still repose."—*Pezuela Ensayo Historico de Cuba*, page
354. " The bones of Cortés were secretly removed from the church
of San Francisco with the permission of his excellency the archbishop, on the 2d July, 1794, at eight o'clock in the evening, in the
carriage of the governor, the Marquis de Sierra Nevada, and were
placed in a vault made for this purpose in the church of Jesus of
Nazareth. The bones were deposited in a wooden coffin inclosed in
one of lead, being the same in which they came from Castilleja de la
Cuesta, near Seville. This was placed in another of crystal, with its
crossbars and plates of silver, and the remains were shrouded in a

The royal palm, one of the most majestic of its species, give a peculiar character to the country in the neighborhood of Havana. It is the *Oreodoxia regia* in my classification of American palms; its tall trunk, slightly swelling near the middle, is from sixty to eighty feet high; the upper portion being of a fresh, shining green color, forms the union and extension of its pedicles, contrasts with the rest of the trunk, which is of a whitish-brown, and shrunken, forming, as it were, two columns, one supporting the other. The royal palm of Cuba has a beautiful pinnatifid leaf, which shoots upward, and bends only near its point.

The description of this palm reminds me of the *Vadgiai* palm, that covers the rocks, and waves its long leaves amid a cloud of spray, at the cataracts of the Orinocco. Those groves of palms that gave me such delight in the vicinity of Havana and Regla. are waning year after year, and the low-grounds which I beheld covered with the waving bamboo, are being drained and cultivated. Civilization advances with rapid pace, and I am told that even in those places yet bare of cultivation, there exists but few remains of their former wild abundance.

winding-sheet of cambric, embroidered with gold, with a fringe of black lace four inches deep.''—*Prescott's Conquest of Mexico*, vol. III. *Appendix*, p. 469.

From the Punta to San Lazaro, from the Cabaña
to Regla, and from thence to Atares, the land is
filled with habitations; those which surround the
bay being of light and elegant construction. The
plan of these houses is drawn, and they are ordered
from the United States, as one would order any piece
of furniture. When the yellow fever prevails at
Havana, the inhabitants retire to these country-
houses, and to the hills between Regla and Guanabacoa, where they breathe a purer air. In the cool
nights, when the boats crossing the bay leave behind
them a long track of phosphorescent light, the inhabitants, who abandon the populous city, find in
these rustic abodes a peaceful and enchanting pri-
vacy. Travellers who wish to judge truly of the
progress of agriculture, should examine the small
patches of maize and other alimentary plants, the
pine-apples in long files in the fields of the Cruz de
Piedra, and the vegetation of the bishop's garden,
which has lately been converted into a most delightful place.

The city of Havana proper is surrounded by walls,
and is about 1,900 yards long by 1060 yards wide;
and yet there are piled in this narrow space 44,000
people, of which 26,000 are blacks and mulattos. A
nearly equal population is gathered in the two
suburbs, Jesus Maria and Salud; but the latter

does not merit the beautiful name it bears (signifying Health); for, although the temperature of the air is lower than in the city, the streets might have been wider, and better laid out.

The Spanish engineer corps has been for the last thirty years making war upon the inhabitants of the suburbs, complaining to the government that the houses are too near the fortifications, and that an enemy might hold possession of them with impunity. But no one has sufficient firmness to raze the suburbs and eject the inhabitants, of which there are 28,000 in that of Salud alone. This ward has increased largely since the great fire of 1802, for although sheds only were at first erected, these have since been replaced by houses.

The inhabitants of the suburbs have laid many plans before the court by which they might be included within the line of the fortifications of the city, and thus obtain a confirmation of their titles to the land which they have hitherto held only by tacit consent.

Some propose that a wide moat shall be cut from the Chaves bridge, near the shambles, to the San Lazaro shore. The distance is about 2550 yards, and the harbor now terminates at the bridge of Chaves, between the navy-yard and the castle of Atares, in a natural brook, the banks of which are

covered with mangroves and reeds. The city would
then have on the west a triple line of fortifications;
first, outward, the works of Principe and Atares,
built upon hills; then the projected moat; and
lastly, the old wall, with its curtain, built by
Count Santa Clara, at a cost of seven hundred˜thou-
sand dollars.

The defence of Havana, on the western side, is of
the greatest importance, for while the city proper
and the southern side of the bay is held, the Morro and
Cabaña castles are impregnable. The first of these
requires a garrison of 800 men, and the second 2,000
men for their defence, provisions for which, and
reinforcements, should the garrison suffer heavy
losses, can be supplied from the city. Several able
French engineers have assured me that an enemy
should begin by taking the city, and then bombard
the Cabaña, which is very strong, but whose
garrison, shut up in the casemates, could not long
resist the sickly climate. The English took the
Morro before they had possession of Havana, but at
that time, the Cabaña, which commands the Morro,
and fort Number 4, had not been built. The castles
of Principe and Atares, and the battery of Santa
Clara, are the most important works on the southern
and western sides of the city.

Population of Havana, including the suburbs,

Salud, Jesus Maria, Horcon, Cerro, San Lazaro, Jesus del Monte, and Regla, in 1810.[1]

	Males.	Females.	Total.
Whites,.........20,686		20,541	41,227
Free colored,....11,631		14,348	25,979
Slaves, ...15,327		13,581	28,908
Total,	47,644	48,470	96,114

The land and naval forces, the monks and nuns, and foreigners not domiciliated (transient persons), are not included in the census of 1810. The figures of this census have been referred to erroneously in works otherwise worthy of credit, as corresponding to the year 1817. The garrison of Havana is usually six thousand men, and the number of foreigners 20,000, so that the population of Havana, with its seven suburbs, doubtless at the present time (1825) exceeds 130,000 souls. The following table shows the increase of Havana and its suburbs between the years 1791 and 1810:

[1] The same by the official census of 1846 :—

	Males.	Females.	Total.
Whites, ...39,531		30,584	70,115
Free colored,....13,231		18,097	31,258
Slaves, ...14,088		12,022	26,110
Total,	66,900	60,588	127,433

	Whites.	F. Colored.	Slaves.	Total.	Proportions of the three classes
1791	23,737	9,751	10,849	44,337	53—22—25
1810	41,227	25,979	28,908	96,114	43—27—30
Increase,	17,490	16,228	17,059	51,777	

Increase of Whites,	73	
" F. Colored,	171	
" Slaves,	165	per cent.
" all classes,	117	

We find that the population has more than doubled in the twenty years from 1791 to 1810, in which time the population of New York, the largest city of the United States, has risen from 33,200 souls to 96,400, and at the present time (1825) reaches 140,000, being consequently a little larger than Havana, and nearly equal to Lyons.

We cannot doubt that the great accumulation of unacclimated foreigners in a confined and populous city augments the mortality, and yet notwithstanding the effects of the yellow fever, in the comparison of births and deaths, the results are much less affected by it than are commonly supposed. When the number of blacks imported is not large, and the activity of trade does not bring together at one time a large number of unacclimated sailors, the number of births very nearly equals the number of deaths.

We present here a statement of marriages, births, and deaths in Havana for five years :

	Marriages.	Births.	Deaths
1813	386	3,525	2,948
1814	390	3,470	3,622
1820	525	4,495	4,833
1821	397	4,326	4,466
1824	397	3,566	6,697

This table, which shows great fluctuations from the unequal influx of foreigners, gives a mean proportion of births to the population as 1 to 33.5; and of deaths as 1 to 33.2, estimating the total population of Havana and suburbs at 130,000 souls. According to recent exact estimates of the population of France, the proportions there are as 1 to 33⅔, and 1 to 39¼; and for Paris from 1819 to 1823 as 1 to 28, and 1 to 31.6.

The principles upon which these calculations are based, are so modified by circumstances in populous cities, and these are of a nature so complicated and variable, we cannot judge of the number of inhabitants by that of births and deaths. In 1806, when the population of the City of Mexico slightly exceeded 150,000, the number of deaths and births there was respectively 5,166 and 6,155, while in Havana with 130,000 souls, the mean number is 3,900 and 3,880.

There are two hospitals in Havana, the public hospital (San Felipe y Santiago), a charitable institution, and the military hospital (San Ambrosio), in both of which the number of patients is quite large. The following table shows their operations :

	San Ambrosio.			San Felipe y Santiago.		
	1814.	1821.	1824.	1814.	1821.	1824.
No. on 1st Jan'y.	226	307	264	153	251	127
Admitted during the year,	4,352	4,829	4,160	1,484	2,596	2,196
Total,	4,578	5,136	4,424	1,637	2,847	2,323
Deaths,	164	225	194	283	743	533
Cured,	4,208	4,623	3,966	1,224	1,948	1,651
Remaining,	206	283	264	130	156	139

The mean of annual deaths in the public hospital is more than 24 per cent., while in the military hospital it is barely 4 per cent. This great difference must not be attributed to the method of treatment employed by the friars of San Juan de Dios, who control the first-named establishment, for though doubtless more yellow fever patients are admitted to the hospital of San Ambrosio, the greater part of the patients received there have slight, and indeed insignificant disorders ; while the public hospital on the contrary, admits the aged, the incurable, and blacks who having but a few months to live, are placed there by their owners to rid themselves of care.

As a general thing, it may be supposed that, with the police improvements, the salubrity of Havana has also improved; but the effects of these changes ,can only be really observed among the native population, for foreigners, who go there from Europe and North America, must suffer from the general influence of the climate, and they will continue to suffer even though the streets were as carefully cleaned as could be desired. The sea-shore has such an influence, that even the natives of the island who reside in the country, far from the coast, are subject to attacks with the yellow fever when they visit Havana.

The markets of the city are well supplied. In 1819 a careful estimate was made of the value of the produce brought daily to Havana by two thousand beasts of burden, and it was found that the consumption of meats maize, yuca, vegetables, rum, milk, eggs, forage, and segars, amounted annually to $4,480,000.

We passed the months of December, January and February, making observations in the vicinity of Havana, and in the beautiful plain of Güines. We found in the Cuesta family, which, with that of Santa Maria, forms one of the largest commercial houses in America, and in the house of Count O'Reilly, the most noble and generous hospitality. We lodged at

the residence of the first-named, and placed our
instruments and our collections of specimens in the
palace of the Count, the broad flat roofs of which
were exceedingly convenient for our astronomical
observations.

[Note.   NAVY-YARD AT HAVANA.

The great advantages which the port of Havana
affords for repairing and building ships were apparent
at an early period.   Its admirable position made it a
port of call for all the ships navigating those seas,
and it was the place of refit and final departure of
the galleons for Spain.   But neither the government
nor private individuals availed themselves of its
abundant timber and naval resources, until about
the year 1626, when the king ordered several vessels
to be built there for the service of the windward
station, of which it was the head-quarters.   After
these were completed the government built no more
vessels there for a long time, although private enterprise continued the business until the king prohibited
the cutting of timber except for the purpose of
building or repairing of houses in the city.

In 1713 Don Augustin de Arriola went to Madrid,
for the purpose of inducing the government to establish a navy-yard at Havana, and proposed to build
there ten ships of the line, which should serve as

convoys for the galleons and fleets from Mexico. He urged upon the court that ships built of the hard woods of Cuba, would be much more durable than those built of European timber, and that they would also be preferable, for the reason that the timber would not splinter in battle, and consequently the ships were safer for the crews. His efforts were for a long time unsuccessful, and it was not until about 1723 the present navy-yard was established, and ship-building permanently undertaken. For nearly three-quarters of a century Havana was the great nursery of the Spanish Armada, and from the year 1724 until 1796, the following ships were built there:—

1724	San Juan .... ship of the line.	50 guns.
1725	San Lorenzo............... "	50 "
1726	San Geronimo (á) El Retiro .. "	50 "
1726	San Antonio (á) El Triunfo ....mail ship.	16 "
1727	N. S. de Guadalupe (á) El Fuerte, ship of the line.	60 "
1727	Santa Barbara (á) la Chata.........corvette.	22 "
1728	San Dionisio (á) El Constante, ship of the line.	54 "
1730	El Marte ....mail ship.	16 "
	El Jupiter .... "	16 "
	Nuestra Señora del Carmen .... three-decker.	64 "
1731	Segundo Constante............ "	60 "
1733	El Africa .... "	60 "
1734	La Europa .... "	60 "
1735	El Asia .... "	62 "
	La Esperanza...................... frigate.	50 "

1735	El Triunfo	corvette.	24 guns.
1736	La America	three-decker.	62 "
1737	La Estrella	corvette.	24 "
738	La Casilla	three-decker.	60 "
	El Dragon	"	60 "
1739	La Bizarra	frigate.	50 "
1740	El Invencible	three-decker.	70 "
	El Glorioso	"	70 "
1743	La Nueva Espana	"	70 "
	El Nuevo Invencible	"	70 "
1745	El Nuevo Conquistador	"	64 "
	Santa Teresa de Jesus	"	64 "
1746	El Nuevo Africa	"	70 "
	El Vencedor	"	70 "
1747	La Flora	corvette.	24 "
	El Tigre	three-decker.	70 "
1749	El Fenix	"	80 "
	El Rago	"	80 "
1750	El Infante	"	70 "
	La Galicia	three-decker.	70 "
	La Princesa,	"	70 "
1757	El Triunfo	brig.	16 "
1758	Santa Barbara	corvette.	18 "
	El Cazador	brig.	18 "
1759	El Astuto	three-decker.	60 "
1760	El Volante	mail-ship.	18 "
1761	El Fenix	corvette.	22 "
	San Ysidro	schooner.	14 "
	San Genaro	three-decker.	60 "
	San Antonio	"	60 "
	San Jose	brig.	14 "
1765	San Carlos	throe-decker.	80 "

1765	San Julian ....schooner.	16 guns
	San Fernando ....three-decker.	80 "
1766	San Joaquin ....schooner.	16 "
	San Jago ....three-decker.	60 "
	San Lorenzo ....schooner.	16 "
1767	San Antonio de Padua............. "	16 ".
	Santa Clara.................... "	10 "
	Santa Ysabol................ "	10 "
	San Luis.....................three-decker.	80 "
	Santa Rosalia ....schooner.	16 "
1768	San Francisco de Paula...........mail-ship.	18 "
1769	San Francisco de Paula........three-decker.	70 "
	La Santissima Trinidada......ship of the line.	112 "
	San José........................schooner.	12 "
1769	San José..................ship of the line.	70 "
1770	Nuestra Señora de Loreto .... .schooner.	12 "
	Santa Lucia ....corvette.	26 "
	El Cayman...................xebec *frigate*.	80 "
1771	San Rafael.................ship of the line.	70 "
	San Pedro Alcantara........ "	62 "
1772	San Juan Bautista. ....brig.	12 "
	San Francisco Xavier................. "	12 "
	Santa Elena ....schooner.	
	San Carlos.....................mail-ship.	18 "
1773	San Miguel ....ship of the line.	70 "
1775	San Roman ....ship of the line.	60 "
	San Julian................dredging lighter.	
	San Salvador de Orta........ "	
1776	Santa Agueda ....frigate.	46 "
	Santa Catalina Martir .... brig.	10 "
1777	Santa Cecilia....................frigate.	46 "
1778	Santa Matilda..................... "	46 "

1778	Santa Teresa ... .schooner.	12 guns
	Nuestra Señora de la O. .. ..frigate.	40 "
1780	Santa Clara........................ "	40 "
	El Bahama ....ship of the line.	70 "
	El Viento ...,.. ....schooner.	14 "
1781	La B——(illegible on record)....... "	
1782	Borja..........................mail-ship.	14 "
	San Pedro.... ....receiving-ship.	
	San Pablo.. .... "	
1786	El Mejicano................ship of the line.	114 "
	Conde de Regla .... "	114 "
	La Guadalupe ....frigate.	40 "
1787	Real Carlos ....ship of the line.	114 "
	La Catalina.................... .frigate.	44 "
1788	San Pedro Alcantara.........ship of the line.	64 "
	Nuestra Señora de la Merced ....frigate.	40 "
1789	San Hermenegildo ....ship of the line.	120 "
	Atocha ....frigate.	40 "
	San Geronimo..............ship of the line.	64 "
1790	El Volador ....brig.	18 "
	El Soberano................ship of the line.	74 "
	Minerva ....frigate.	44 "
	Saeta................ ....brig.	18 "
1791	Dredging ship. ... No 1.	
	" ....., " 2.	
	4 Dredging lighters " 1, 2, 3, and 4.	
	El Infante Don Pelayo ....ship of the line.	74 "
	La Ceres..........................frigate.	40 "
1792	La Gloria......................... . "	44 "
1793	El Principe de Asturias.......ship of the line.	120 "
1794	San Antonio.. ... .brig.	18 "
1796	La Anfitrite ....frigate.	44 "

Forming a total of

Ships of the line	51	3642
Frigates	16	684
Corvettes	7	160
Mail-ships	7	116
Brigs	9	136
Schooners	14	164
Receiving ships	2	
Dredging "	2	
" lighters	6	
	114	4902

A few years since, the labors at the navy-yard of Havana were resumed; a machine shop was established, and a steamer, a sloop of war, and several smaller vessels were built; but they were again suspended by a royal decree, and the fixed machinery and ship-timber were taken to Cadiz. Vessels of the station are now only repaired here. The reason assigned for this is that ship-building in Cuba deprives the labor of the mother country of employment.]

CHAPTER II.

PHYSICAL ASPECT.

Figure of the island but lately known—Area according to Lindenean
and Ferrer—According to Bauzá—According to "Cuadro Estadistico"—Comparative area—Length and width—Importance of
Batabanó—Comparative territorial power—Geological character
—Mountains—Face of the country—Elevation—Noted hills—
Eastern portion—Gold-washing—Formation of western and central portion—Güines—Soil—Hills of San Juan—Caverns—Modern
formation—Shore at Havana—Roaring banks explained—Relative
age of strata—Fresh water on the cays—Origin—Vicinity of
Havana — Guanabacoa — Serpentine — Petroleum — Botany of
Guanabacoa—Mineral springs—Reflections on geology — Earthquakes—Fertile lands—Beauty of vegetation—Soils, how distin-
guished—Rivers—Springs—Lands near Havana. [NOTE.—Imperfect state of geological knowledge in Cuba—Known metal and
mineral productions—Coal analyzed—Celebrated mineral springs
—Analysis of tobacco lands in the Vuelta de Abajo.]

As the shores of the island of Cuba are covered
with cays and reefs through more than two-thirds
of their extent, and the navigable channels lie outside of these obstructions, the true figure of the
island was for a long time unknown. Its width,

particularly between Havana and Batabanó, has been exaggerated, and it is only since the Hydrographic bureau at Madrid, the best establishment of its kind in Europe, has published the labors of Capt. José del Rio and Lieut. Ventura Barcaiztegui, that its area has been calculated with any degree of accuracy. The figure of the Isle of Pines, and of the southern coast between the port of Casilda and Cape Cruz (inside of the Doce leguas cays), has been laid down very differently in our several maps.

Lindeneau, in view of the publications of the Bureau previous to 1807, had stated the area of Cuba, without the neighboring small islands, to be 2,255 square geographical leagues (fifteen to a degree), and 2,318 with the islands that surround it, which is equivalent to 4,102 square maritime leagues of twenty to the degree. Señor Ferrer, with somewhat different data, does not make it exceed 3,848 square maritime leagues.

In order to give in this work the most exact results possible in the present state of astronomical observations there, I have induced Señor Bauzá, who honors me with his friendship, and whose name has become celebrated through his great and valuable labors, to calculate the area in accordance with the new map of the island on four sheets, which he will soon complete. This learned geographer has acced-

ed to my request, and found (in June, 1825), the
superficial area of Cuba, without the Isle of Pines,
to be 3,520 square maritime leagues, and 3,618 with
that island.[1]

By this calculation, which has been twice made,
it appears that the Island of Cuba is one-seventh
smaller than has been hitherto supposed; that it is
one-third larger than St. Domingo, and only one-
eighth smaller than England exclusive of Wales. If
the entire archipelago of the Antilles possesses an
area equal to one-half that of Spain, Cuba alone
nearly equals in superficial extent all the other Greater
and Lesser Antilles together. Its greatest length
from Cape San Antonio to Cape Maysi (on a line
running from W. S. W. to E. N. E., and then from
W. N. W. to E. S. E., through the island,) is 227 leagues.
Its greatest width, from Maternillo point to the mouth
of the river Magdalena, near Tarquino peak (from

[1] The official "Cuadro Estadistico" of 1846 states the area as
follows:

Cuba	34,283 square mi es.
Isle of Pines.........................	810 " "
Small islands adjacent	970 " "
	36,013 square miles.

Which exceeds Señor Bauzá's calculation for Cuba by 2,553 square
miles, and is five times greater than Massachusetts, and more than
one-half the area of all the New England states.

N. to S.), is 37 leagues. The mean width of the island between Havana and Puerto Principe, being about four-fifths of its length, is 15 leagues.

In the most cultivated part, between Havana and Batabanó, the island is only 8½ leagues across. This proximity of the northern and southern shores at this point makes the port of Batabanó of great importance both for commerce and for military defence. Among the great islands of the globe, that of Java, from its shape and area (4,170 square leagues), most resembles Cuba. The coast-line of Cuba extends 520 leagues, of which 280 correspond to the southern shore between Cape San Antonio and Cape Maysi.[1]

That the territorial power of Cuba, as comparing with the rest of the Antilles, may be better seen, we present the following table :—

	Extent in sq. leagues.	Population.	Pop. to sq. league.
Cuba according to Bauzá,	3,615	715,000	197
Haïti " Lindeneau,	2,450	820,000	334
Jamaica,	460	402,000	874
Puerto Rico,	322	225,000	691
Great Antilles,	6,847	2,147,000	313
Lesser Antilles,	940	696,000	740
Whole Archipelago,	7,787	2,843,000	365

[1] The "Cuadro Estadistico" of 1846 states the shore-line at 573 leagues, of which 301 correspond to the south, and 272 to the north coast.

More than four-fifths of the land of Cuba is low
and its surface covered with secondary and tertiary
formations, through which granitic-gneis, syenite,
and euphotide rocks have protruded.

At present we have no very exact idea of the
geognostic character of the country, nor of the relative age or nature of its soils. We only know that
the highest group of mountains is in the extreme
southeastern portion of the island, between Cape
Cruz, Cape Maysi and Holguin. The ridge known
as the *Sierra del Cobre*, situate northwest of the
city of St. Jago de Cuba, is said to be more than
7,600 feet high.[1] According to this supposition, the
hills of this ridge are higher than the Blue Mountains of Jamaica, and the peaks of Banquillo, and
Banaste of St. Domingo. The *Sierra de Tarquino*,
fifty miles west of the city of St. Jago, belongs to the
same group with the *Sierra del Cobre*.

A chain of hills runs through the island from
E.S.E. to N.N.W., approaching the southern coast

[1] The *Sierra del Cobre* is supposed by some travellers to be visible
from the shore of Jamaica, but most probably it is from the northern slope of the Blue Mountains. In the first case, its height would
exceed ten thousand feet, supposing a refraction of one-twelfth
Certain it is, that the mountains of Jamaica are visible from the
summit of the hills of Tarquino.—*Patriota Americana, Vol.* ii.
p. 282.—H.

between Puerto Principe and Trinidad; while more to the wést, toward Alvarez and Matanzas, the sierras of Gavilan, Camarioca, and Madruga approach the northern shore. While travelling from the mouth of the river Guaurabo to Trinidad, I saw the hills of San Juan, which form peaks more than 1,900 feet high, whose slopes incline with great regularity to the south. This calcareous group is seen very clearly from Cay de Piedras. The coasts of Jagua and Batabanó are very low, and I believe there is no hill exceeding 1,275 feet in height, except the Pan of Guajaibon, west of the meridian of Matanzas.

The face of the interior of the island is gently undulating, like that of England, and is not more than 280 to 380 feet above the level of the sea.[1] The objects seen at the greatest distance, and best known to navigators, are the "Pan of Matanzas,"[2] which is a truncated cone like a small monument in shape; the "Arcos de Canasí," which are seen between Puerto Escondido and Jaruco, like small segments of a circle; the "Table land of Mariel,"

[1] The village of Ubajay, about fifteen miles distant from Havana, S. 25° W., is 242 feet above the sea. The summit line of Bejucal, at the Taverna del Rey, is 305.7 feet.—H.

[2] 1,255 feet high. At sea I have found the "Arcos de Canasi" to be 732 feet high.—H.

the "Maiden's Paps," and the "Pan de Guajaibon."[1]
This level of the limestone formation of Cuba,
declining toward the northwest, indicates the submarine union of these rocks with the similar low
lands of the Bahama Islands, Florida, and Yucatan.

As observation has been limited to Havana and
its immediate neighborhood, we should not be surprised at the profound ignorance displayed in
relation to the geognosy of the Sierra del Cobre.
Don Francisco Ramirez, a traveller, who had been a
pupil of Proust, and was well versed in the chemical
and mineralogical sciences, informed me that the
western part of the island is granitic, and that he
had found there gneiss and primitive slate. From
these granitic formations have probably arisen the
alluvial sands mixed with gold which were worked
with so much zeal during the early years of the
conquest, to the great misfortune of the natives, and
vestiges of them are still found in the rivers of
Holguin and Escambray; these alluvial sands are
found generally in the vicinity of Villa Clara, Santi
Espiritu, Puerto Principe, Bayamo, and the Bay of

[1] 2484 feet high. Further west, on the northern coast, we have the
"Sierra de los Organos," and "Sierra de Rosario," and on the southern
coast, the "Sierra de Rio Puerco."—H.

Nipe.[1] Perhaps the abundance of copper spoken of by the *conquistadores* of the sixteenth century, at which time the Spaniards observed the natural productions of America better than they did in subsequent ages, is due to the formations of hornblende slate, and slate *de transition*, mixed with diorite and euphotide rocks analogous to those I found in the hills at Guanabacoa.

The central and western parts of the island contain two formations of compact limestone; one with sandy clay, and the other with gypsum. The first of these presents (I will not say from its relative age, or its superposition, which I do not know, but from its composition and appearance) some similarity with the formation of the Jura. It is white or of a light yellow ochre color, brittle, sometimes conchoidal

[1] This supposition of ancient riches is not unlikely, and if we wonder at the small product of the gold washings in our days in Cuba and St. Domingo, at the same places where, in former times, considerable sums were found, we should remember that in Brazil, the yield of the gold washings has fallen from 6,600 kilogrammes to less than 595, between the years 1760 and 1820. The lumps of gold, several pounds in weight, which have been found in our days, in Florida and the two Carolinas, demonstrate the primitive richness of the entire valley of the Antilles, between the island of Cuba and the Appalachian chain; but it is natural that the yield of the gold washings should diminish with much greater rapidity than that of the working of subterraneous veins.—H.

and sometimes smooth, and lies in very thin layers
with nodules of pyrogeneous silex, often hollow
(Rio Canimar, two leagues east of Matanzas), and
petrifications of pecten, cardites, terrebratules, and
madrepores, which are not so much dispersed
through the mass as gathered in banks. I found no
layers of petrified oolites, but there were porous and
almost hollow strata, between the potrero of Count
de Mopox and the port of Batabanó, similar to the
spongy strata presented by the jurassic limestone at
Franconia, near Dondorf, Pegnitz, and Tumbach·
Yellow cavernous strata, with holes, from three to
four inches diameter, alternate with others, entirely
compact and less abundant in petrifactions.[1]

The chain of hills which bounds the valley of
Güines upon the north, uniting with the hills of
Camoa and the "Tetas de Managua," appertain to the
second variety, which is of a reddish white color,
and almost lithographic, like the jurassic limestone at
Papenheim. The compact and the cavernous strata
contain brown, ochreous veins of iron, and perhaps
the red soil so esteemed by the coffee planters, arises
from the decomposition of some of these superficial

[1] As the western portion of the island has no deep fissures, this
alternation is observed while travelling from Havana to Batabanó;
the deeper strata crop out with an inclination of 30° to 40° N.E. as
one advances.—H.

layers of oxidized iron, mixed with silica and clay, or with a red sandy marl lying upon the limestone.[1] All this formation I shall call Güines limestone, to distinguish it from another much more modern formation in the hills of San Juan, near Trinidad; whose peaks remind me of the limestone mountains of Caripe, in the vicinity of Cumaná. It contains also great caverns near Matanzas and Jaruco. I have not learned that any fossil bones have been found in them. This frequency of caverns, in which the rains accumulate and the brooks disappear, sometimes causes great disasters.[2] I believe the gypsum of Cuba is not found in the tertiary, but in the secondary formations. It is worked in many places east of Matanzas, at San Antonio de los Baños, where it contains sulphur, and in the cays off San Juan de los Remedios.

We should not confound with this Güines (jurassic) limestone, sometimes porous and sometimes compact, another formation, so modern, that we may believe it still grows in our own time. I speak of the conglomerate limestone which I have observed in the cays or small islands lining the coast between Batabanó and the Bay of Jagua, south of the Zapata swamp,

[1] Sand and iron-sand.—H.

[2] As in the case of the ruin of the old tobacco mills of the royal monopoly.—H.

principally on Cay Bonito, Cay Flamenco, and Cay de Piedras. By the soundings, we know that these are rocks rising precipitously twenty or thirty fathoms from the bottom. Some are level with the sea, and others rise from one and a half to two feet above the surface. Sharp fragments of white coral and shells (cellularia), two or three cubic inches in size and cemented with grains of quartz-sand, are there found. All the inequalities of these rocks are covered with made earth, in which, with a lens, we can distinguish nothing but detritus of shells and coral. This tertiary formation corresponds, without a doubt, to that of the coasts of Cumaná, Carthagena, and the Gran Terre de la Guadalupe, of which I have spoken in my geognostic view of South America.

Messieurs Chamisso and Guaimard have lately thrown much light upon the formation of the coral islands of the southern seas. While we see at Havana, at the foot of the Punta fort, upon the shore of cavernous rocks,[1] covered with verdant

---

[1] The surface of these shores, blackened and worn by the waves, presents conical ramifications such as are found in lava currents. The change of color caused by the waters is the effect of manganese, the presence of which is known from the detritus. As the sea enters the fissures of the rock and a cavern at the base of the Morro Castle, it compresses the air and forces it out with an extraordinary noise, which explains the phenomenon of the roaring banks so well known

ulves and living polipfers, large masses of madrepore, and other lithophite corals, enclosed in the texture of the rock, there is reason to admit that all this limestone rock of which the island of Cuba is in great part composed, is the effect of an uninterrupted operation of nature through the action of organic productive forces and partial destruction, and which continues in our time in the bosom of the ocean. But this appearance of recent formation soon disappears, when we leave the shore, or when we remember the series of coral rocks which the formations of different epochs enclose, the muschelkalk, the limestone of the Jura, and the *calcaire grossier* of Paris.

The same coral rocks of the Punta castle are found in the highest mountains in the interior of the country, accompanied by petrifactions of bivalve shells, very different from those which at present exist on the shores of the Antilles. Without wishing to assign with certainty to the limestone formation of Güines a determinate place in the scale of formations, I entertain no doubt as to the relative antiquity of this rock with the conglomerate limestone of the cays, situate south of Batabanó, and east of the Isle of Pines. The globe has experienced great revolutions between the epochs of these two formations,

to navigators between Jamaica and San Juan de Nicaragua, and near the Island of St. Andrew.—H.

one of which contains the great caverns of Matanzas
and the other is daily augmented by the accumulation of fragments of coral and quartz sand. The
latter of these formations seems to rest on the south
part of Cuba, sometimes on the Güines (jurassic)
limestone, as in the Jardinillos, and at others (toward
Cape Cruz) immediately upon the primitive rock.
In the Lesser Antilles the coral has covered the
volcanic products.

Many of the cays of Cuba contain fresh water, and
I have found excellent water in the centre of Cay de
Piedras. When we remember how extremely small
these islands are, we can hardly believe that those
ponds of fresh water are rain water that has not
evaporated. Perhaps they arise from a submarine
communication between the limestone formation of
the shore, and that which has served as a base for
the collection of the lithophites : so that the fresh
water of Cuba rises by hydrostatic pressure through
the coral rock of the cays, as is the case in the bay
of Jagua, where fountains spring forth in the salt
water, and are the resort of the Manatí.

East of Havana the secondary formations are
traversed by Syenite and Euphotide rocks, grouped
in a singular manner. The southern side of the bay,
as well as the northern (the hills of the Morro and
Cabaña), are of jurassic limestone ; but on the east-

ern side of the two arms—Guanabacoa and Guassa-
bacoa, the entire formation is *de transition*. Passing southward, we find syenite near Marimelena,
composed in a large degree of hornblende, and in part
decomposed with a little quartz, and a reddish white
feldspar, which is sometimes crystallized. This beautiful syenite, whose masses incline to the northwest,
alternates twice with serpentine, and the intercalated
strata of this stone is seventeen or eighteen feet thick.

Further south toward Regla and Guanabacoa,
there is no syenite, and the entire surface is covered
with serpentine, in hills from 200 to 250 feet high,
running from east to west. This rock is much
fissured, its exterior being of a bluish brown color,
covered with detritus of manganese, and the interior
of leek or asparagus green traversed by small veins
of asbestos. It contains neither granite nor hornblende, but metallized diallage is disseminated through
the mass. The serpentine breaks sometimes in leaves,
sometimes in scales, and this was the first instance
of my finding metallized diallage within the tropics.
Many of the pieces of serpentine have magnetic
poles, and others have a texture so homogeneous,
and so firm a polish, that from a distance they may
be mistaken for pitchstone, (pechstein). It is desirable that these beautiful masses should be used in
the arts as is done in many places in Germany.

Approaching Guanabacoa, the serpentine is found
traversed by veins twelve or fourteen inches thick,
filled with fibrous quartz, amethyst, and rich mam-
milated stalactiform chalcedony; perhaps chryso-
prase will some day be found with them. Among
these veins some copperish pyrites appear, which
are said to be mixed with an argentiferous grey
copper ore. I found no vestiges of this grey copper
ore, and it is probably metallized diallage, which,
for ages have given the hills of Guanabacoa the
reputation of containing much gold and silver.
Petroleum exudes in some places through the
fissures in the serpentine.[1] Springs are frequent

[1] Are there in the bay of Havana other petroleum springs than
those of Guanabacoa, or should we suppose that the liquid *betun*,
used by Sebastian Ocampo, in 1508, when he careened his vessels
here, have become dry? It was this that attracted the attention of
Ocampo to the port of Havana, when he gave it the name of
"Puerto de Carenas." It is said that abundant petroleum springs
have been found in the eastern part of the island, between Holguin
and Mayari, and on the shores of St. Jago de Cuba. A small island,
Siguapa, has recently been found, near Point Hicacos, which
presents to the eye solid, terreous petroleum only; this mass recalls
to the mind the asphaltum of Valorbe, in the limestone of the Jura.
Does the serpentine formation of the Guanabacoa recur in the Ruby
hill, near Bahia Honda? The hills of Regla and Guanabacoa
present to the botanist, at the feet of royal palms, Xatrofa
panduraefolia; X. integerrima Jacq; X. fragrans; Petiveria
alliacia; Pisonia loranthoides; Lantana involucrata; Russella

there, the water of which contains a little sulphureted hydrogen and deposits oxide of iron. The baths
of Bareto are very agreeable, but their temperature
is very nearly that of the atmosphere. The geognostic constitution of that group of serpentine is worthy
of particular attention from its isolation, its veins,
its connection with the syenite, and its elevation
through formations filled with petrified shells.

A feldspar, with base of soda (compact feldspar),
forms, with diallage, the euphotide and serpentine
rocks; with hypersthene it forms hypersthenite; with
hornblende, diorite; with augite, dolerite and basalt;
and with granite, eclogite. These five rocks dispersed throughout the globe, charged with oxidized
iron and mixed with sphene, have in all probability
a similar origin. In the euphotides two formations
are easily distinguishable; one wanting hornblende,
even when it alternates with hornblende rocks (Joria
in Piedmont, Regla in Cuba), and abounding in pure
serpentine, metallized diallage, and sometimes jasper
(Tuscany, Saxony); and the other heavily charged

sarmentosa; Ehretia havanensis; Cordia globosa; Convolvulus
pinnatifidus; C. calycinus; Bignonia lepidota; Lagascea mollis
Car.; Malpighia cubensis; Triopteris lucida; Zanthoxylum; Pie-
rota; Myrtus tuberculata; Mariscus havanensis; Andropogon ave-
naceus Schrad.; Olyra latifolia; Chloris cruciata; and a large
number of Banisteria, whose gilded flowers adorn the scene.—*See
our Florula Cuba insula*, in the *Nov. Genera Spec.*—H.

with hornblende often giving way to diorite, without jasper, in layers, and sometimes containing rich veins of copper (Silesia, Mussinet in Piedmont, Pyrenees, Parapara in Venezuela, Copper mountains of Western America). This last-named formation of the euphotides is that which, from its mixture with diorite, blends with hypersthenite, in which, in Scotland and Norway, strata of true serpentine is sometimes found. No volcanic rocks of a more recent epoch, as, for example, trachytes, solerite, and basalt, have been discovered in the island of Cuba; and I am not aware if there are any in the other Great Antilles, whose geognostic constitution differs essentially from that of the series of limestone and volcanic islands, that extends from the island of Trinidad to the Virgin Isles.

Earthquakes are much less disastrous in Cuba than in Puerto Rico and Haiti, and are experienced most in the eastern part between Cape Maysi, St. Jago de Cuba, and Puerto Principe. Perhaps there extends toward those regions some lateral action from the great fissure which is believed to extend across the granitic tongue of land between Port au Prince and Cape Tiburon (in St. Domingo), in which entire mountains were sunk in 1770.[1] The cavern-

---

[1] Dupuget, in the "Diario de Minas," vol. I. p. 58, and Leopold de Buch, Phy. Beschr. der Canar. Inseln., 1825, p. 403.—H.

ous texture of the limestone formations which I have just described, the great inclination of its strata, the small width of the island, the frequent absence of trees in the plains, and the proximity of the moun- tains, where they form an elevated chain near the southern coast, may be considered- as the principal causes of the want of rivers, and of the absence of moisture which are experienced, particularly in the western part of Cuba. In this respect Haiti, Jamaica, and many other of the Lesser Antilles which have volcanic peaks covered with woods, are much more gifted by nature.

The lands most celebrated for their fertility are those of the districts of Jagua, Trinidad, and Mariel. The valley of Güines owes its reputation in this respect entirely to its artificial irrigation by means of canals. Notwithstanding the absence of deep rivers and the unequal fertility of the soil, the island of Cuba presents on every hand a most varied and agreeable country from its undulating character, its ever-springing verdure, and the variety of its vegeta- ble formations. Two kinds of trees with large flexible and shining leaves, five species of palms (the Royal palm, or Oreodoxia regia, the Coco comun, the Coco crispa, the Coripha miraguama, and the C. mari- tima), and small bushes, ever laden with flowers, adorn the hills and vales. The Cecropia peltata

marks the humid places, and we might believe that
the entire island was originally a forest of palms
and wild lime, and orange trees. These last, which
have a small fruit, are probably anterior to the
arrival of the Europeans,[1] who carried there the
agrumi of the gardens, which rarely exceed ten or
fifteen feet in height.

The lime and the orange do not usually grow
together, and when the new settlers clear the land
they distinguish the quality of the soil according as
it bears one or other of these social plants; and the
soil that bears the orange is preferred to that which
produces the small lime. In a country where the
operations of the sugar plantations have not been so
well perfected that they need no other fuel than the
bagasse, this progressive destruction of the small
clumps of wood is a real calamity. The arid nature
of the soil is increased in proportion as it is stripped
of the trees which serve to shield it from the hot rays
of the sun, and whose leaves radiating their caloric

---

[1] The well-informed inhabitants state, with pride, that the cultivated orange brought from Asia preserves its size and all the properties of its fruit when it becomes wild. (This also is the opinion
of Señor Gallesio.—"Traité du Citrus," p. 32). The Brazilians do
not doubt that the small bitter orange, which bears the name of
naranjo do terra, and is found wild far from the habitations, is of
American origin.—*Caldcleugh's Travels in South America*, vol. I.
p. 25.—H.

against an ever clear sky, cause a precipitation of the
watery vapor from the cooled air.

Among the few rivers worthy of notice, we may cite
that of Güines, the waters of which it was intended, in
1798, to turn into the canal for light draught navigation, that was to have crossed the island under the
meridian of Batabanó; the Almendares or Chorrera,
whose waters are carried to Havana by the *zanja de
Antonelli;* the Cauto, north of the city of Bayamo;
the Maximo, which rises east of Puerto Principe;
the Sagua la Grande, near Villa Clara; the Palmas,
which empties into the sea opposite to Cay Galindo;
the smaller rivers of Jaruco and Santa Cruz, between
Guanabo and Matanzas, which are navigable for some
miles from their mouths, and facilitate the embarca-
tion of sugar; the San Antonio, which, like many
others, disappears in the caverns of the limestone
rock; the Guaurabo, west of the port of Trinidad;
and the Galafre, in the fertile Filipinas district,
emptying into the Bay of Cortés.

The southern side of the island is most abundant in
springs, where, from Jagua to Point Sabina, a distance of forty-six leagues, the country is a continuous
swamp. The abundance of water that filtrates
through the fissures of the stratified rock is so great,
that from the hydrostatic pressure, springs are found
in the sea at some distance from the coast.

The lands in the district of Havana are not the most fertile, and the few sugar plantations that were near the capital have been turned into grazing farms, and fields of corn and forage, the demand for the city making them very profitable. Agriculturists in Cuba recognize two classes of land which are often found intermixed like the squares of a chess-board; the black or brown soil, which is argillaceous, and highly charged with sooty exhalations, and the red land, which is a strong soil and mixed with oxide of iron. Although the black land is generally preferred for the cultivation of the sugar cane, because it preserves its moisture better, and the red land for the coffee tree, yet many sugar plantations have been made in the red lands.

[NOTE. The geology of Cuba is still very imperfectly known, no systematic examination of its surface having been made, and the board appointed to compile the "Cuadro Estadistico" of 1846 stated, that in regard to this portion of their labors they could do little more than reproduce the remarks accompanying the "Cuadro" of 1827. Besides the observations of Baron Humboldt, Don Francisco Ramirez, and Don Ramon de la Sagra have been the principal scientific writers on this subject; the former having travelled through a portion of the eastern department, early in the present century, and the latter having resided several years previous to 1833, at Havana, where he was director of the Botanic Garden. From these sources we obtain the following information in relation to its mineral resources.

Gold.—During the earlier years of settlement gold washings and mines were worked by native Indians, and Pedro Martir de Angleria, one of the most learned of the early historians of America, states that Cuba was more rich in gold than St. Domingo. The knowledge of the mines has been lost, though one is said to exist near Trinidad; but small quantities of gold are still washed out from the sands of the rivers Damují and Caonao, emptying into the bay of Jagua, the Sagua la Grande and Agabama, near the Escambray hills, the Saramaguacan, running into the bay of Nuevitas, and brooks in the vicinity of Holguin, Bayamo and Nipe. It is said to have been found formerly near San Juan de los Remedios.

Silver has been found in combination with copper near Villa Clara, yielding seven and a half ounces to the hundred pounds of ore.

Quicksilver is said to have been extracted in former times from the arid savannas of the Copey hacienda, near San Juan de los Remedios.

Copper abounds through a great part of the island,

7

and more than one hundred mines have been entered, in accordance with the law, at the Treasury department, though but few of them are worked at present. The ores of those near St. Jago de Cuba have yielded at one time seventy-five per cent. of copper.

Iron has been found in several places, among which are Nueva Filipina, Bahia Honda, Jaruco, Villa Clara, Santi Espiritu, Holguin, St. Jago de Cuba, and Baracoa. An analysis of a vein near St. Jago de Cuba yielded twenty-six per cent. of metal.

Plumbago is found in combination with iron, near St. Jago de Cuba.

Copperas is also found in the same vicinity.

Antimony, with *Lead*, is said to exist near Holguin.

Talc and *Amianthus* exist in the vicinity of Trinidad, Holguin, and Santi Espiritu.

Ochre is found at Manzanillo, St. Jago de Cuba, Santa Maria del Rosario, and Guanabacoa.

Chrome.—Deposits of this pigment have been worked near Holguin.

Chalk exists at Manzanillo, and near Moron.

Grindstone and *Whetstone*, in great varieties, are found at Nueva Filipina, and in many places in the eastern part of the island.

Coal has been often sought, but hitherto without

success. Veins of solidified asphaltum (*betun*) exist in many places. Several analyses have been made of this substance; that of Guanabacoa, near Havana, giving—

Volatile matter	63
Carbon	35
Ashes and residuum	2
	100

It burns with great flame and smoke, but cakes very much, and leaves a light, bulky coke. Its specific gravity is 1.14. Specimens from the veins near Guanabo were analyzed by Señor Sagra, in 1828, giving—

Volatile matter	28
Carbon	60
Ashes and residuum	12
	100

Specific gravity, 1.18.

Marble is found in great abundance in many places.

Loadstone exists also in large quantities.

Moulding sand, of fine quality, abounds in Nueva Filipina.

Mineral springs are found in many parts of the island, some of which have great renown among the inhabitants for their sanative properties. The most celebrated are the following:

San Diego, forty leagues S.W. from Havana. The water of the two springs, *Tigre* and *Templado*, comes from the earth with a temperature of 95° Far. Their analysis by Señor Esteves gave to one pound of water, 0.46 grains sulphureted hydrogen, 10.5 sulphate of lime, 1. hydrochlorate of magnesia, and 1. carbonate of magnesia.

Madruga, fifteen leagues S.E. from Havana. The water is of lower temperature than that of San Diego, but similar in its qualities.

Guanabacoa, one league from Havana. There are several springs here: that of *Tarraco* being similar to the waters of Madruga; *Baño de la Condesa*, of like qualities, but more highly charged with sulphureted hydrogen; the water of the *Amber* well (*de succino*), so called from its amber taste and odor, is esteemed as a stomachic tonic; the baths of *Barreto, Español, Cassanova,* &c., are highly recommended. No analysis has been made of these waters, but they are all more or less charged with magnesia, nitre, and oxide of iron.

Mayajigua, nineteen leagues from San Juan de los Remedios. The water of this spring has a very great local reputation. It presents the phenomenon of being about fifteen degrees warmer in the morning and evening than at other hours.

Guadalupe, sixteen leagues from Santi Espiritu;

not analyzed, but similar to the waters of Guana-bacoa.

Camujiro, two and a half leagues from Puerto Principe. The water is highly charged with iron, and being very tonic, is highly esteemed.

The waters of several streams in Cuba are reputed to possess mineral qualities, and to produce medi-cinal effects upon bathers.

We close this imperfect view of the geology and mineral resources of Cuba with the following analysis of some of the celebrated Tobacco lands, as given by Don Ramon de la Sagra.

San Diego de los Baños, two localities :—

Organic matter	18.40	23.20
Silica	70.80	68.20
Lime	0.40	4.60
Alumina	0.40	vestiges.
Oxide of iron	10.00	4.00
	100.00	100.00

Vuelta de Abajo, two localities :

Organic matter	9.60	4.60
Silica	86.40	90.80
Lime	0.00	vestiges.
Alumina	0.68	3.40
Oxide of iron	1.92	1.20
Loss	1.40	0.00
	100.00	100.00

CHAPTER III.

CLIMATE.

General remarks—Mean temperature—Means of heat and cold—
Summer solstice—Peculiarities of winter—Compared with Macao
and Rio Janeiro—Fires not needed—Hail—General remarks
—Anomalies of vegetation—The pine of Cuba—Identity with that
of Mexico—Temperature in the interior and at Havana—Comparison with Cumaná—Ice—Snow never seen in Cuba—Sudden changes
at Havana—Internal heat of the earth—Oscillations of thermometer and barometer connected—Barometrical altitudes—Hurricanes.
—[NOTE.—Hurricanes of 1844 and 1845—Rain gauge and Hygrometer—Atmospherical phenomena—Cloudy and fair days—Effect
of climate on vegetation.]

THE climate of Havana is that which corresponds
to the extreme limit of the torrid zone ; it is a tropical
climate, in which the unequal distribution of heat
through the various seasons of the year presages the
transition to the climates of the temperate zone.

Calcutta (N. lat. 22° 34'), Canton (N. lat. 23° 8'),
Macao (N. lat. 22° 12'), Havana (N. lat. 23° 9'), and
Rio Janeiro (S. lat. 22° 54'), are places whose
location at the level of the ocean and near the
tropics of Cancer and Capricorn, being equi-dis-

tant from the equator, makes them of the greatest importance in the study of meteorology. This science can advance only by the determination of certain *numerical elements*, which are the indispensable basis of the laws we wish to discover. As the appearance of vegetation on the confines of the torrid zone and under the equator is the same, we are accustomed vaguely to confound the climates of the zones comprised between the 0° and 10°, and 15° and 23° of latitude. The region of the palm, the banana, and the arborescent grasses, extends far beyond the tropics, but we should err in applying the result of our observations on the limit of the torrid zone, to the phenomena we may observe in the plains under the equator.

It is important to establish first, in order to correct these errors, the means of temperature for the year and the months, as also the oscillations of the thermometer at different stations under the parallel of Havana; and by an exact comparison with other places equally distant from the equator, Rio Janeiro and Macao, for example, to demonstrate that the great decline of temperature which has been observed in Cuba, is owing to the descent and irruption of the masses of cold air which flow from the temperate zones toward the tropics of Cancer and Capricorn.

The mean temperature of Havana, as shown by

excellent observations made through four years, is
25°.7 centigrade (78°.25 Fahrenheit), being only 2°
C. (3°.6 F.) lower than that of the regions of
America under the equator. The proximity of the
sea increases the mean temperature of the coasts, but
in the interior of the island, where the northern
winds penetrate with equal force, and where the
land has the slight elevation of 250 feet, the mean
temperature does not exceed 23° C. (73°.4 F.), which
is not greater than that of Cairo and all Lower Egypt.

The difference between the mean temperature of
the hottest month and that of the coldest is 12° C.
(21°.6 F.) in Havana, and 8° C. (14°.4 F.) in the
interior, while at Cumaná, it is barely 3° C. (5°.4
F.) July and August, which are the hottest
months attain in Cuba a mean temperature of 28°.8
C. (83°.8 F.), and perhaps even 29°.5 C. (85°. 1 F.),
as under the equator.

The coldest months are December and January;
their mean temperature is 17° C. (62°.6 F.) in the
interior of the island, and 21° C. (69°.8 F.), in
Havana, that is, from 5° C. to 8° C. (9° F.), (14°.4 .
F.) less than during the same months under the
equator, but yet 3° C. (5°.4 F.) higher than that of the
hottest month in Paris.

As regards the extremes touched by the centigrade
thermometer in the shade, the same fact is observed

near the limits of the torrid zone that characterizes the regions nearer the equator (between 0° and 10° of north and south latitude); a thermometer which had been observed in Paris at 38°.4 (101° F.), does not rise at Cumaná above 33° (91°.4 F.); at Vera Cruz it has touched 32° (89°.6 F.), but once in thirteen years. At Havana, during three years, (1810–1812), Señor Ferrer found it to oscillate only between 16° and 30° (61° and 86° F.). Señor Robredo, in his manuscript notes, which I have in my possession, cites as a notable event that the temperature in 1801 rose to 34°.4 (94° F.), while in Paris, according to the interesting investigations of Mons. Arago, the extremes of temperature between 36°.7 and 38° (97°.9 and 100°.4 F.) have been reached four times in ten years, (1793–1803.)

The great proximity of the days on which the sun passes the zenith of those places situate near the limit of the torrid zone, makes the heat at times very intense upon the coast of Cuba, and in all those places comprised between the parallels of 20° and 23½°, not so much as regards entire months as for a term of a few days. In ordinary years the thermometer never rises in August above 28° or 30° C. (82°.4 or 86° F.), and I have known the inhabi_tants complain of excessive heat when it rose to 31° C. (87°.8 F.)

It seldom happens in winter that the temperature falls to 10° or 12° C. (50° to 53°.6 F.), but when the north wind prevails for several weeks, bringing the cold air of Canada, ice is sometimes formed at night, in the interior of the island, and in the plain near Havana. From the observations of Messrs. Wells and Wilson, we may suppose that this effect is produced by the radiation of caloric when the thermometer stands at 5° C. (41° F.), and even 9° C. (48°.2 F.) above zero. This formation of a thick ice very near the level of the sea, is more worthy the attention of naturalists from the fact, that at Caraccas (10° 31′ N. lat.), at an elevation of 300 feet, the temperature of the atmosphere has never fallen below 11° C. (41°.8 F.); and that yet nearer to the equator we have to ascend 8,900 feet to see ice form. We also observe that between Havana and St. Domingo, and between Batabanó and Jamaica, there is a difference of only 4° or 5° of latitude, and yet, in St. Domingo, Jamaica, Martinique, and Guadalupe, the minimum temperature in the plains is from 18°.5 to 20°.5 C. (65°.3 to 68°.9 F.)

It will be interesting to compare the climate of Havana with that of Macao and Rio de Janeiro, one similarly situated near the northern extreme of the torrid zone, but on the eastern shore of Asia, and the other near the southern limit of the torrid zone, on the

eastern shore of America. The means of temperature
at Rio Janeiro are deduced from three thousand five
hundred observations made by Señor Benito Sanchez
Dorta ; those of Macao from twelve hundred observations which the Abbé Richenet has kindly sent me.

Mean.	Havana, N. lat. 28° 9'.	Macao, N. lat. 22° 12'.	Rio Janeiro, S. lat. 22° 54'.
For the year,	78°.26 F.	73°.94 F.	74°.30 F.
" " hottest month,	83°.84 F.	83°.12 F.	80°.96 F,
" " coldest "	69°.98 F.	61°.88 F.	68° F.

The climate of Havana, notwithstanding the
frequent prevalence of north and northwest winds,
is warmer than either that of Macao or Rio
Janeiro. The first named of these places is somewhat cold, because of the west winds which prevail
along the eastern shores of the great continent. The
proximity of very broad stretches of land, covered
with mountains and high plains, makes the distribution of heat through the months of the year, more
unequal at Macao and Canton, than in an island
bordered by sea-shores upon the west, and on the
north by the heated waters of the Gulf Stream. Thus
it is that at Canton and Macao the winters are much
more severe than at Havana.

The mean temperatures of December, January,
February, and March, at Canton, in 1801, were be-

tween 15° and 17°.3 (59° and 62° F.); at Macao, between 16°.6 and 20° (61°.9 and 68° F.); while at Havana they were generally between 21° and 24°.3 (69°.8 and 75°.7); yet the latitude of Macao is one degree south of that of Havana, and the latter city and Canton are on the same parallel, with a difference of one mile, a little more or less. But although the isothermal lines, or lines of equal heat, are convex toward the pole in the *system of climates of Eastern Asia*, as also in the *system of climates of Eastern America*, the cold on the same geographical parallel is greater in Asia.[1] The Abbé Richenet, who used the excellent *maximum* and *minimum* thermometer of Six, has observed it to fall even to 3°.3 and 5° (38° and 41° F.), in the nine years, from 1806 to 1814.

At Canton, the thermometer sometimes falls to 0° C. (32° F.), and from the radiation of caloric, ice is formed on the roofs of the houses. Although this excessive cold never last more than one day, the English merchants residing at Canton light fires

[1] The difference of climate is so great on the eastern and western shores of the old continent, that in Canton, lat. 23°.8′, the mean annual temperature is 22°.9 (63°.2 F.), while at Santa Cruz de Teneriffe, lat. 28°. 28′, it is 23°.8 (74°.8 F., according to Buch and Escolar. Canton, situate upon an eastern coast, enjoys a continental climate. Teneriffe is an island near the western coast of Africa.—H.

during the months of November, December, and January, while at Havana fires are never needed.

Hail of large size frequently falls in the Asiatic countries round Canton and in Macao, while at Havana fifteen years will pass without a single fall of hail. In all three of these places the thermometer will sometimes stand for hours between 0° and 4° C. (32° and 39°.7 F.); yet notwithstanding (which seems to me more strange), it has never been known to snow; and although the temperature falls so low, the banana and the palm grow as well in the neighborhoods of Canton, Macao, and Havana, as in the plains immediately under the equator.

In the present state of the world it is an advantage to the study of meteorology, that we can gather so many numerical elements of the climates of countries situate almost immediately under the tropics. The five great cities of the commercial world—Canton, Macao, Calcutta, Havana, and Rio Janeiro, are found in this position. Besides these, we have in the Northern hemisphere, Muscat, Syene, New Santander, Durango, and the Northern Sandwich Islands; in the Southern hemisphere—Bourbon, Isle of France, and the port of Cobija, between Copiapo and Arica, places much frequented by Europeans, and which present to the naturalist the same advantages of position as Rio Janeiro and Havana.

Climatology advances slowly, because we gather by chance the results obtained at points of the globe where the civilization of man is just beginning its development. These points form small groups, separated from each other by immense spaces of lands unknown to the meteorologist. In order to attain a knowledge of the laws of nature regulating the distribution of heat in the world, we must give to observation a direction in conformity with the needs of a nascent science, and ascertain its most important numerical data. New Santander, upon the eastern coast of the Gulf of Mexico, probably has a mean temperature lower than that of the Island of Cuba, for the atmosphere there must participate, during the cold of winter, in the effects of the great continent extending towards the northwest.

On the other hand, if we leave the *system of climates of Western America,* if we pass the lake, or, more strictly speaking, the submerged valley of the Atlantic, and fix our attention upon the coasts of Africa, we find that in the *cis-Atlantic system of climates* upon the western borders of the old continent, the isothermal lines are again raised, being convex towards the pole. The tropic of Cancer passes between Cape Bojador and Cape Blanco, near the river Ouro, upon the inhospitable confines of the desert of Sahara, and the mean temperature

of those countries is necessarily hotter than that of
Havana, for the double reason of their position upon
a *western* coast, and the proximity of the desert,
which reflects the heat, and scatters particles of sand
in the atmosphere.

We have already seen that the great declinations
of temperature in the island of Cuba are of so short
duration, that neither the banana, the sugar-cane,
nor the other productions of the torrid zone, suffer
the slightest detriment. Every one is aware how
readily plants, that have great organic vigor, sustain
momentary cold, and that the orange-trees in the
vicinity of Genoa resist snow-storms and a degree
of cold not lower than 6° or 7° C. below zero (21°.2
or 19°.4 F. above zero).

As the vegetation of Cuba presents an identity of
character with that of regions near the equator, it is
very extraordinary to find there, even in the plains,
a vegetation of the colder climates, identical with
that of the mountains of Southern Mexico. In other
works, I have called the attention of botanists to
this extraordinary phenomenon in the geography of
plants. The pine (*pinus occidentalis*), is not found
in the Lesser Antilles, and according to Mr. Robert
Brown, not even in Jamaica (between 17¾° and 18°
of latitude), notwithstanding the elevation of the
Blue Mountains in that island. Further north only

do we begin to find it, in the mountains of St.
Domingo, and throughout the island of Cuba, which
extend from 20° to 23° of latitude. There, it attains ·
a height of sixty or seventy feet, and what is still
more strange, the pine and the mahogany grow side
by side in the plains of the Isle of Pines. The pine
is also found in the southeastern part of Cuba, on
the sides of the Cobre Mountains, where the soil is
arid and sandy.

The interior plain of Mexico is covered with this
same class of coniferas, if we may rely upon the
comparison made by Bonpland and myself, with the
specimens we brought from Acaguisotla, the snow
mountain of Toluca, and the Cofre of Perote, for
these do not seem to differ specifically from the
pinus occidentalis of the Antilles, as described by
Schwartz. But these pines, which we find at the
level of the sea in Cuba, between the 20° and 22° of
latitude, and only upon its southern side, do not
descend lower than 3,200 feet above that level upon
the Mexican continent, between the parallels of $17\frac{1}{4}$°
and $19\frac{1}{4}$°. I have even observed that on the road
from Perote to Jalapa, on the eastern mountains of
Mexico, opposite to Cuba, the limit of the pines is
5,950 feet, while on the western mountains, between
Chilpancingo and Acapulco, near Cuasiniquilapa,
two degrees further south, it descends to 3,900 feet,

and at some points, perhaps, even to the line of 2,860 feet.

These anomalies of position are very rare under the torrid zone, and depend probably less on the temperature than on the soil. In the system of the migration of plants, we should suppose that the *pinus occidentalis* of Cuba had come from Yucatan, before the opening of the channel between Cape Catoche and Cape San Antonio, and not, by any means, from the United States, although the coniferous plants abound there, for the species of whose geography we are treating has not yet been found in Florida.

The following table exhibits the results of observations of temperature, made at Ubajay, in Cuba.

	1796.	1797.	1798.	1799.
January,	65° F.	64° F.	68° F	61° F.
February,	72	66	69	63
March,	71	64	68¼	64
April,	74	68	70	68
May,	78½	77	73	76
June,	80	81	83	85
July,	82½	80	85	87
August,	83	84	82	84
September,	81	81½	80	86
October,	78	75½	79½	73
November,	75	70	71	61
December,	63	67½	60	59
Mean,	75°.2	73°.2	74°.2	71°.4

The village of Ubajay, as I have before said, lies about five maritime leagues from Havana, in a plain 242 feet above the level of the sea. The partial mean temperature of December, 1795, was 18°.6 C. (65°.84 F.); that of January and February, 1800, had varied from 13°.8 C. (56°.84 F.) to 18°.9 C. (66°.12 F.) by Nairne's thermometer.

MEAN OF OBSERVATIONS AT HAVANA.

	1800.	1810–12.
January,	——	70° F.
February,	——	72°
March,	70° F	79°
April,	72°.9	78°.6
May,	77°.9	82°.2
June,	86°	82°.7
July,	86°.5	82°.9
August,	82°.9	83°.4
September,	79°	82°.6
October,	79°.9	79°.5
November,	72°.	75°.6
December,	74°.8	70°
Mean,	78°.3	78°.3

Comparison betweeen the mean temperature in the interior and on the shore of Cuba and at Cumaná, in South America. See following table.

	Ubajay, int. of Cuba.	Havana coast.	Cumaná N. lat 10° 27'.
December to February	64°.4 F.	71°.2	80°.4
March to May	71°.2	79°.2	83°.7
June to August	81°.8	83°.3	82°.0
September to November	74°.8	78°.6	82°.6
Mean	73°.2	78°.3	81°.7
Coldest months	62°.0	70°.0	79°.2
Hottest "	83°.5	83°.4	84°.4

At Rome, N. lat. 41° 53'—Mean temp......... 59° F.

    "   "   Hottest month...... 77°.0

    "   "   Coldest "   .... 42°.3

During the last fifteen days of the year 1800, I observed the centigrade thermometer almost constantly between 10° and 15° (50° and 59° F). At the hacienda Rio Blanco (in Cuba), it fell in January to 7°.5 C. (45°.5 F.) In the country near Havana, on a hill 318 feet above the level of the sea, water has frozen, the ice being several lines in thickness. Señor Robredo informed me of this fact, which again occurred in December, 1812, after a prevalence of very strong northerly winds for nearly a month.

As it snows in the flat countries of Europe, when the thermometer is several degrees above zero, (32° F.), it is surprising that in no part of this island, nor even in the hills of San Juan, nor in the high mountains of Trinidad, has it ever been known to

snow; and frost is known only on the crests of these
hills and of the Copper Mountains. We must suppose
that other conditions than the rapid fall of temperature in the upper regions of the air are needed for it
to hail and snow.

I have stated elsewhere that it has never been
known to hail at Cumaná, and very rarely in
Havana, happening only once in fifteen years, during
violent electrical explosions and S.S.W. winds. At
Kingston, Jamaica, the fall of the thermometer at
sunrise to 20°.5 (69° F.), is cited as an extraordinary
phenomenon. In that island we must ascend the
Blue Mountains to the height of 7,325 feet, to see
it fall to 8°.3 (47° F.) in the month of August. At
Cumaná, 10° N. lat., I have not known the thermometer to to fall to 20°.8 (69°.4 F.).

Changes of temperature occur very suddenly in
Havana. In April, 1804, the variation of the thermometer in the shade, within the space of three
hours, was from 32°.2 to 23°.4 C. (89° to 74°.1 F.),
that is, 9° C. (16°.2 F.), which is very considerable
in the torrid zone, and twice as great as the variation found on the coast of Colombia, further south.
The inhabitants of Havana (N. lat. 23° 8') complain
of cold when the temperature falls rapidly to 21° C.
(69°.8 F.), and in Cumaná (N. lat. 10° 28'), when it
falls to 23° C. (73°.4 F.) In April, 1804, water sub-

jected to rapid evaporation of heat, and which was deemed very cool, stood at 24°.4 C. (75°.9 F.), while the mean temperature of the air was 29°.3 C. (84°.7 F.)

A collection of many careful observations of the internal heat of the earth on the confines of the torrid zone, would be interesting. In the caverns of the limestone formation, near San Antonio de Beita (Cuba), and in the springs of the Chorrera river, I have found it to be between 22° and 23° C. (71°.6 and 73°.4 F.), and Señor Ferrer observed it at 24°.4 C. (75°.9 F.) in a well one hundred feet deep. These observations, which perhaps have not been made under advantageous circumstances, show a temperature of the earth much lower than that of the air, which is seen to be 25°.7 C. (78°.3 F.) at Havana, and 23° C. (73°.4 F.) in the interior of the island, at an elevation of 255 feet. These results do not conform with observations made at other places in the temperate and glacial zones. Do the very deep currents which carry the water of the poles towards the regions of the equator, diminish the internal temperature of the earth in islands of narrow breadth? We have treated this delicate question in relating our experience in the caverns of Guacharo, near Caripe. It is stated that in the wells of Kingston, Jamaica, and the low lands of Guadalupe, the thermometer has been observed at 27°.7, 28°.6, and 27°.2 C. (81°9, 83°.5, and 81° F.), consequently at a temperature equal to that of the air at these places.

The great changes of temperature to which countries on the borders of the torrid zone are subject, have a connection with certain oscillations of the barometer, which are not observed in the regions near the equator. At Havana, as well as at Vera Cruz, the regular variations of atmospheric pressure experienced at determinate hours of the day, are interrupted when strong northerly winds prevail. I have observed that the barometer in Cuba generally stands, when the sea-breeze is blowing, at 0.765, and that it fell to 0.756, and even lower, when the south wind blew.

It has been stated in another place, that the mean barometrical altitudes of the months when the barometer is highest (December and January), vary in respect to the months when the barometer is lowest (August and September), from 7 to 8 millimetres, that is to say, almost as much as at Paris, and five or six times more than at the equator, and 10° north and south latitude.

Mean altitude.—December..... 0.76656 or 22.1 Cent. of T.
     "   January ...... 0.76809 " 21.2 "
     "   July.......... 0.76453 " 28.5 "
     "   August........ 0.76128 " 28.8 "

During the three years 1810–1812, when Señor Ferrer took the mean altitudes, the extreme variation on those days when the mercury rose or fell most in the barometer, did not exceed thirty millimetres. In order to exhibit the accidental oscillations of each month, I present here the table of observations in 1801, in the hundredth parts of an English inch, according to the manuscript notes of Don Antonio Robredo.

	Maximum.	Minimum.	Mean.	Mean. temperature.
January,	30.35	29.96	30.24	14.5 R.
February,	30.38	30.01	30.26	15.6
March,	30.41	30.20	30.32	15.5
April,	30.39	30.32	30.35	17.2
May,	30.44	30.38	30.39	19.4
June,	30.36	30.33	30.34	22.2
July,	29.38	29.52	30.22	22.4
August,	30.26	30.12	30.16	22.8
September,	29.18	29.82	30.12	21.0
October,	30.16	30.04	30.08	18.6
November,	30.18	30.09	30.12	16.5
December,	30.26	30.02	30.08	12.1

Hurricanes are less frequent in Cuba than in St. Domingo, Jamaica, and the Lesser Antilles situate east and south of Cape Cruz; for we should not confound the violent north winds with the hurricanes, which most generally blow from the S.S.E, or the

S.S.W.   At the time I visited the island of Cuba, no hurricane had occurred since the month of August, 1774, for the gale of the 2d November, 1796, was too light to be so called.

The season when these violent and terrible movements of the atmosphere occur in Cuba, during which a furious wind prevails, varying to every point of the compass, and frequently accompanied by lightning and hail, is during the last of August, the month of September, and particularly that of October.   In St. Domingo and the Caribbean Isles, those most feared by seamen occur during July, August, September, and the first fifteen days of October.   Hurricanes are most frequent there in the month of August, so that this phenomenon manifests itself later as we proceed toward the west.

Violent southeast winds also prevail at Havana, during the month of March.   No one in the Antilles acknowledges that the hurricanes have their regular periods.   Seventeen occurred from 1770 to 1795, while from 1788 to 1804, none were experienced in Martinique.   In the year 1642, three occurred.

It is worthy of notice that at the two extremities of the long cordillera of the Antilles (the S.E. and N.W.), hurricanes are least frequent.   The islands of Tobago and Trinidad, happily, never experience them, and in Cuba, these violent ruptures of the atmospheric equilibrium rarely occur. When they do happen, the destruction they cause is greater at sea than on the land, and more upon the southern and southeastern coast, than upon the northern and northwestern. 1n 1527, the famous expedition of Panfilo de Narvaez was partly destroyed by one in the harbor of Trinidad de Cuba.

[Note.—Since the visit of Baron Humboldt to Cuba, in the beginning of the present century, only two hurricanes have been experienced there. The first of these occurred on the 4th and 5th of October, 1844. It began about ten o'clock on the evening of the 4th, and continued with great violence until daylight, when the point of greatest descent of the barometer, 28.27, was observed. From that time, it subsided, and the torrents of rain began to cease, but the wind continued to blow with great violence until 10 A.M. This storm passed over all the zone of country comprised between Bahia Honda and Sierra Morena on the north, and Galafre and Cienfuegos on the south side of Cuba. One hundred and fifty-eight vessels were wrecked in the harbors and on the coasts, and one hundred and one lives were lost. The crops suffered severely, and 2,546 houses were destroyed. The second hurricane occurred in the following year, and was more destructive than the preceding one. It began about midnight of the 10th October, and increased in violence, with torrents of rain and spray, until 10 30 A.M. of the 11th, when the barometer had fallen to 27.06, the lowest point it has ever been known to touch in Cuba. Its ravages extended over nearly the same extent of country with that of 1844, but its greatest violence was confined to a circle of about forty miles radius round Havana. Two hundred and twenty-six vessels were lost, 1,872 houses were blown down, 5,051 partially destroyed, and 114 persons perished. During both of these hurricanes, the wind veered to every point of the compass, and the salt spray was carried fifteen or twenty miles inland, blackening vegetation as though fire had passed over it.— (Arboleya, *Manual de la Isla de Cuba.*)

To the foregoing admirable view of the climate of Cuba, by Baron Humboldt, we can only add the following tables and remarks from Don Ramon de la Sagra's " Historia Fisica, Politica y Natural de la Isla de Cuba." The indications of the rain-gauge are in English inches, and the hygrometer is expressed by Deluc's scale.

RAIN FALLEN AT HAVANA, AND MONTHLY MEAN OF HYGROMETER.

	1811.	1812.	1813.	1814.	1815.	Mean.	Hygrom.
January ..	0.00	7.14	0.20	1.70	3.67	3.17	15.12
February .	0.00	1.98	0.54	3.08	2.17	1.94	56.08
March	1.70	3.15	0.48	2.90	0.25	1.70	53.71
April.....	3.60	2.40	0.00	5.90	0.15	2.41	52.04
May......	2.05	2.63	5.55	3.67	3.10	3.40	51.84
June	11.26	0.00	5.85	6.50	6.59	5.94	55.42
July	8.33	2.75	6.31	8.42	2.35	5.63	56.34
August ...	2.89	2.57	4.35	1.75	1.61	2.66	54.44
September	7.27	1.61	4.37	5.40	5.17	4.75	54.60
October ..	0.90	5.41	8.92	0.73	8.71	4.93	55.40
November	1.40	0.75	1.30	0.62	4.93	1.80	56.10
December	1.45	0.36	2.38	0.90	1.44	1.43	54.95
Totals ..	40.85	31.35	39.75	41.57	40.14	39.76	54.67

"Notwithstanding the frequency of rain during the hot season, that is during the months of July August, and September, these months do not present the greatest number of cloudy days. The rains of summer, although copious, are of short duration, and those days on which showers do not fall, are in general perfectly cloudless. It may almost be said that during these months no clouds are to be seen in the atmosphere, except while the shower is falling, while in the other months cloudy days sometimes occur without rain. Days during which the heavens

are completely clouded are extremely rare in Cuba :
we give from our diary the mean of our observations
for each month :

	Cloudy days.	Clear and partially cloudy days.
January	5	26
February	8	20
March	7	24
April..............	5	25
May....	8	23
June	6	24
July	6	25
August	6	25
September ....,	7	23
October......	7	24
November....	8	22
December	7	24
Total	80	285

"These tables will give some idea of the beauty
of the sky in these regions, and of its effect upon the
life and luxuriant growth of vegetation. A high
temperature, moderated by great evaporation, which
pours through the atmosphere a continuous torrent of
watery vapors, presents the most favorable conditions
for the development of an admirable vegetation;
which again contributes, on its part, to maintain the
humidity of the atmosphere—soul of its exuberant life.
Thus it is that through all seasons of the year the

fields and forests of Cuba preserve their verdure; but
it is principally at the beginning of summer, during
the rainy season, that all nature there seems to be
transformed to flowers."

CHAPTER IV.

GEOGRAPHY.

Banks and reefs round Cuba—North coast—South coast—Territorial
divisions — Judiciary—Ecclesiastical — Politico-military — Public
Finances—Proposed new division—Present dividing line of bishoprics—Number of parishes—Popular territorial divisions—First
governor—[NOTE, Maritime subdivision.]

I MIGHT have cited, among the causes of the low
temperature in Cuba, during the winter months, the
numerous shoals that surround the island, on which
the temperature of the sea is greatly diminished,
partly by the polar currents which seek the abysses
of the tropical ocean, and partly by the mixing of
the surface and the deep waters on the steep sides of
the banks; but this cause of fall in the temperature
is partly compensated by that river of warm water
(the Gulf Stream), which bathes the whole extent of
the northwestern shore of Cuba, and whose rapid
flow is often delayed there by the northern and
northwestern winds.

The chain of shoals that surrounds this island, and

which appears like a shading in our maps, is fortunately broken in many places; and these interruptions afford to commerce a free access to the shore. The parts of the island which are least dangerous, and most free from reefs, sandbanks, and rocks, are the southeastern side, between Cape Cruz, and Cape Maysi (72 maritime leagues), and the northwestern, between Matanzas and Cabañas (28 leagues). On the southeastern side, the proximity of high mountains makes the shore bold; there we find the harbors of St. Jago de Cuba, Guantanamo, Baitiquiri, and, doubling Cape Maysi, Baracoa. This last-named port was the first one settled by Europeans.

The north side of the island, from Cape Mulas, N.N.W. of Baracoa, to the port of Nuevitas, is equally free from banks and reefs. East of Cape Mulas, ships find excellent anchorage in the bays of Tanamo, Cabonico, and Nipe, and, west of that cape, in the bays of Sama, Naranjo, Padre, and Nuevas Grandes. The uninterrupted series of cays lining the old Bahama Channel, and extending from Nuevitas to Point Hicacos, a distance of ninety-four leagues, commences near the bay of Nuevas Grandes, almost under the same meridian with the beginning of the Buena Esperanza Banks, on the south side, which are prolonged to the Isle of Pines.

The narrowest part of the old Bahama Channel is

between Cape Cruz and Cay Romano, where it is
barely five or six leagues wide. The shoalest part
of the Great Bahama Banks is also in this vicinity.
The islands and parts of this bank not covered by
water (Long Island, Eleuthera, &c.), are very exten-
sive; and, should the level of the ocean fall twenty
or thirty feet, an island larger than Haiti would
appear here upon its surface. The chain of cays
and reefs that lines the shore of Cuba is so broken
that it affords small but clear channels to the
harbors of Guanaja, Moron, and Remedios.

Passing through the old Bahama Channel, or,
more properly speaking, through San Nicholas'
Channel, between Cruz del Padre and the cays of
Cay Sal-bank, many of which have springs of fresh
water, we again find a safe coast from Point Hicacos
to Cabañas bay, with the harbors of Matanzas, Puerto
Escondido, Havàna, and Mariel. Further west,
beyond the harbor of Bahia Honda, the possession
of which might well tempt any maritime power at
war with Spain, the chain of shoals and reefs (Santa
Isabel and Colorados), again commences, and continues, without interruption, to Cape San Antonio.

On the south side, the shore from this cape to
Point Piedras and the Bay of Cortés is very bold,
and gives no soundings; but between Point Piedras
and Cape Cruz, nearly all of the coast is covered

with shoals, of which the Isle of Pines is but a part, not covered by water. The western portion is known as the Jardines and Jardinillos—the eastern as Cay Breton, Cays de Doce Leguas, and the bank of Buena Esperanza. The navigation of all this extent of southern coast is dangerous, except from the Bay of Cochinos to the mouth of the river Guaurabo.

The resistance offered by the elevated land of the Isle of Pines to the ocean currents, may be said to favor at once the accumulation of sand and the labors of the coral insect, which thrives in still and shallow water. In this extent of one hundred and forty-five leagues of coast, but one-seventh of it, lying between Cay de Piedras and Cay Blanco, a little west of the harbor of Casilda, presents a clear shore with harbors; these are the roadstead of Batabanó, and the bays of Jagua and Casilda. East from the latter port, toward the mouth of the river Cauto and Cape Cruz (inside of Cay de Doce Leguas), the shore, which is full of springs, is very shallow and inaccessible, and almost entirely uninhabited.

In Cuba, as formerly in all the Spanish possessions of America, we find those subdivisions of the country which have so puzzled modern geographers; these are the Ecclesiastical, the Politico-Military, the

Public Finances, and the Judiciary. We shall not speak of the latter, as the island has but one *Audiencia*, which was established at Puerto Principe, in 1797, its jurisdiction extending from Baracoa to Cape San Antonio.[1]

The ecclesiastical division of two bishoprics dates from 1788, when Pope Pius VI., created the first bishop of Havana. The island of Cuba, together with Louisiana and Florida, was formerly a part of the archbishopric of St. Domingo, and from the time of its discovery constituted but one bishopric, which was founded at Baracoa, in 1518, by Pope Leo X. This bishopric was translated to St. Jago de Cuba, in 1522, but the first bishop, Friar Juan de Ubite, did not reach his diocess until 1528. In the beginning of the present century' (1804), the bishop of St. Jago was created archbishop.

In the Politico-Military government, the island is divided into two departments, both subordinate to the captain-general. That of Havana comprises, besides the capital, the districts of Nueva Filipinas, Cuatro Villas (Trinidad, Santi Espiritu, Villa Clara, and San Juan de los Remedios), and Puerto Prin-

[1] Another *Audiencia* was established at Havana, in 1839, and the island divided into two judiciary districts. The *Audiencia* of Puerto Principe was subsequently abolished, and its jurisdiction united with that of Havana.

cipe. The captain-general, who is also governor of the department of Havana, appoints a lieutenant-governor for each of the several districts. The jurisdiction of the captain-general extends also as *Corregidor* to eight municipalities, being the cities of Matanzas, Jaruco, San Felipe y Santiago, and Santa Maria del Rosario, and the towns of Guanabacoa, Santiago de las Vegas, Güines, and San Antonio de los Baños.

The department of Cuba comprises the district of that name, and those of Baracoa, Holguin, and Bayamo. The boundaries of these two departments are not the same with those of the ecclesiastical divisions; as, for instance, the district of Puerto Principe, with seven parishes, was subject, in 1814, to the governor of Havana, and to the bishop of St. Jago de Cuba. In the census of 1817–20, Puerto Principe is united, with Bayamo and Baracoa, to the department of Cuba.[1]

We have only to consider the third subdivision,

[1] In 1827, the Politico-Military constitution was re-organized, and the island was divided into three departments—Western, Central, and Eastern—with some alterations in the districts, required by the increase of population. This subdivision continued until 1850, when the old form of two departments was re-established—the district of Puerto Principe being placed under the jurisdiction of the governor of the Eastern department.

which appertains entirely to the administration of
the revenue. By a royal decree of 23 March 1812,
three intendencies or provinces were created, viz.:
Havana, Puerto Principe, and St. Jago de Cuba,
which extend, from east to west, about 90, 70, and
65 leagues, respectively. The intendant of Havana
retains the title and prerogatives of sub-delegate-
superintendent-general of the royal treasury of
Cuba. Under this subdivision, the intendancy of
St. Jago de Cuba comprises that district, and those
of Baracoa, Holguin, Bayamo, Gibara, Manzanillo,
Jiguaní, Cobre, and Las Tunas. That of Puerto
Principe comprises the district of that name, and
those of Nuevitas, Jagua, Santi Espiritu, San Juan
de los Remedios, Villa Clara, and Trinidad. The
intendancy of Havana comprises all that part of the
island lying west of the district of Cuatro Villas.
The intendant resides at Havana.

When the island shall become more advanced in
population and agriculture, it would seem to be more
convenient and more in conformity with the historic
recollections of the times of the conquest, that it
should be divided into five departments; that of the
Vuelta Abajo, extending from Cape San Antonio to
the beautiful town of Guanajay and Mariel; *Havana*,
from Mariel to Alvarez; *Cuatro Villas*, from Alvarez to Moron; *Puerto Principe*, from Moron to the

river Cauto; and *Cuba*, from the Cauto to Cape Maysi.

The dividing line of the two bishoprics runs from the mouth of Santa Maria Creek, on the south coast, to Point Judas, opposite Cay Romano, on the north. During the short time that the rule of the Spanish constitution extended to Cuba, the ecclesiastical division also served for that of the representative districts of Havana and St. Jago.

The diocess of Havana contains forty parishes, and that of St. Jago twenty-two, which, having been established at a time when the island contained only cattle or grazing farms, are very large, and ill-adapted to the wants of the present population.[1]

The most common and popular territorial divisions, with the people of Havana, are the *Vuelta de Arriba* and the *Vuelta de Abajo*, lying east and west of the meridian of Havana. The first captain-general of the island was Don Pedro Valdez, appointed in 1601. Sixteen governors had preceded him, the first of whom was the famous *Poblador* and *Conquistador, Diego Velazquez*, a native of Cuellar, in Spain, who was appointed by Diego Colon, at that time admiral and governor of St. Domingo.

[1] Under the present ecclesiastical arrangement, the diocess of Havana contains one hundred and sixteen, and that of St. Jago forty-one parishes.

[NOTE.—There is now another territorial subdivision in Cuba, known as the Marine department. The island is divided into five districts, which are Havana, Trinidad, San Juan de los Remedios, Nuevitas, and St. Jago de Cuba. The head-quarters of the Spanish naval power in America is established at Havana.]

CHAPTER V.

POPULATION.

Its political importance—Former census—Population in 1825
—Compared with other Antilles—Relative proportions of races
in slave countries—Reflections—Why slaves have not diminished since 1820—Proportions of free, and slaves, and of
sexes—Fears on cessation of slave trade—Why unfounded—
Distribution of population in 1811—Free colored seek the towns
—Relative density—Census of 1775—Of 1791—Their contradictions—Corrections—Motion in Spanish Cortes for abolition of
slavery—Remonstrance from Cuba—Census of 1817—Is not complete—Mode of estimating increase—Relative increase of classes
—Several causes of increase—Rate—Excessive between 1791 and
1810—Unequal distribution of classes—[NOTE.—Census of 1827,
1841, and 1846—Reasons for distrusting that of 1846—Supposed
decrease of slaves—Its improbability—Reasons therefor—Increase
of slaves—Annual rate of total increase—Present population.]

In the preceding chapters, we have examined the
area, geological constitution, and climate of a country opening a vast field to civilized man. That we
may duly appreciate the influence which the richest
of the Antilles, under the stimulus of great natural
elements of power, may some day exercise in the
political balance of insular America, let us compare

her present population with that she can maintain upon her 8,600 square leagues of country, the greater part of which is very fertile under the abundant tropical rains, and is still unconscious of the presence of man.

Three successive, but very inexact enumerations have stated the population as follows :—

In 1775,	170,862.
1791,	272,140.
1817,	630,980.

According to this last census, there were, in the island, 290,021 whites, 115,651 free colored and 225,268 slaves. These results agree very well with the interesting papers on this subject, laid before the Spanish Cortes in 1811, by the Ayuntamiento of Havana, in which the approximate population was stated to be 600,000 souls, viz. :—274,000 whites, 114,000 free colored, and 212,000 slaves.

If we take into consideration the several omissions that occurred in the census of 1817, the number of slaves imported (there were entered, at the Havana custom-house, during the three years, 1818–19, and 20, more than 41,000), and the ratio of increase of the white and free colored population, in the eastern part of the island, as shown in the two census of 1810 and 1817, we shall find the probable population of Cuba, at the close of 1825, to be—

Whites,	325,000
Free colored,	130,000
Slaves,	260,000
Total,	715,000[1]

Consequently, the population of Cuba at the present time (1825), is very nearly equal to that of all the English Antilles, and almost double that of Jamaica. The relative proportion of the inhabitants, according to race and state of civil liberty, presents the most extraordinary contrasts in those countries where slavery has taken great root. The following statement shows these proportions, and gives rise to deep and grave reflections.

COMPARATIVE POPULATION OF THE ANTILLES AND THE UNITED STATES.

	Population.	White.	Free colored.	Slaves.	Ratio.
Cuba,	715,000	325,000	130,000	260,000	46 : 18 : 36
Jamaica,	402,000	25,000	35,000	342,000	6 : 9 : 85
English Antilles,	776,500	71,350	78,350	626,800	9 : 10 : 81
All the Antilles,	2,843,000	482,600	1,212,900	1,147,900	17 : 43 : 40
U. States,	10,525,000	8,575,000	285,000	1,665,000	81 : 3 : 13

[1] The official census of 1827 states the population in that year as follows :—

Whites,	311,051
Free colored,	106,494
Slaves,	256,942
Total,	704,487

We perceive by this table, that the free population in Cuba is .64 of the whole population; in the English Antilles it is barely .19. In all the Antilles the colored population (blacks and mulattoes, free and slave), forms a total of 2,360,000, or .83 of the entire population.

If the legislation of the Antilles, and the condition of the colored population, does not soon experience some salutary change, and if discussion without action is continued, the political preponderance will will pass into the hands of that class which holds the power of labor, the will to throw off the yoke, and valor to undergo great privations. This bloody catastrophe will occur as the necessary consequence of circumstances, and without the free negroes of Haiti taking any part whatever, they continuing always the isolated policy they have adopted. Who shall dare to predict the influence which an *African Confederation of the Free States of the Antilles*, lying between Colombia, North America and Guatemala, might have in the politics of the New World?

The fear that such an event might be realized, undoubtedly operates more powerfully upon the minds of men, than do the principles of humanity and justice; but in all the islands the whites believe themselves to be the strongest; for simultaneous action on the part of the negroes, seems to them impossible, and every change, or concession made to a population subject to servitude, is deemed to be cowardice. But it is not yet too late, for the horrible catastrophe of St. Domingo happened because of the inefficiency of the government. Such are the illusions which prevail with the great mass of the colonists of the Antilles, and form an obstacle to improvement in the state of the negroes in Georgia and the Carolinas. The island of Cuba may free herself better than the other islands from the common shipwreck, for she has 455,000 freemen, while the slaves number only 260,000; and she may prepare gradually for the abolition of slavery, availing herself for this purpose, of humane and prudent measures. Do not let us forget that since Haiti became emancipated, there are already in the Antilles more free negroes and mulattoes than slaves. The whites, and more particularly the free blacks, who may easily make common cause with the slaves, increase rapidly in Cuba.

The slave population of Cuba would have diminished with great rapidity since 1820, had it not been for the fraudulent continuance of the slave-trade with Africa. If this infamous traffic should cease entirely, through the advance of civilization, and the energetic will of the new States of Free America, the servile population would diminish largely for some time, because of the existing disproportion between the sexes, and because many would continue to attain their liberty. This decrease would not cease until the relative proportion of births and deaths should compensate even for the slaves freed.[1]

The whites and free colored comprise nearly two-thirds of the entire population of the island; and by their increase we already perceive, in part at least, the relative decrease of the slave population. The The proportion of women to men among this class, exclusive of the mulatto slaves, is as 1 to 4 on the sugar estates; in the whole island it is as 1 to 1.7; in the cities and haciendas, where the negro slaves are servants, or hire their time from their masters, it is as 1 to 1.4, and even (in Havana for example) as 1 to 1.2.

The prognostications which some too lightly make, of a decrease in the entire population of the island upon the actual cessation of the African slave-trade, (not its legal cessation which occurred in 1820); of the impossibility of continuing the cultivation of sugar on a large scale; of the approach of a time when the agricultural interest of Cuba will become reduced to the planting of coffee and tobacco, and the breed-

---

[1] See note at the end of this chapter.

ing of cattle, are founded upon arguments which do not seem to me sufficiently conclusive.

They do not take into consideration the fact, that but one-sixth of the total number of slaves are on the sugar plantations, many of which are not sufficiently stocked with hands, and consequently debilitate their slaves by-frequent night-labor, while the problem of the *pro ratâ* increase of the total population of Cuba, when the importation of negroes from Africa shall have ceased entirely, is based upon elements so complicated, upon such various *compensations* of effect upon the white, free-colored, and slave rural population on the sugar, coffee, and tobacco plantations; the slaves on the grazing farms, and those who are servants, laborers, and mechanics, in the cities, that we should not anticipate such mournful presages, but wait until positive statistical data have been obtained.

The spirit in which the censuses have been taken, even the oldest, that of 1775, for example, marking the distinctions of age, sex, race, and state of civil liberty, is worthy of the highest praise. The means of execution only have been wanting, for the government has recognized how important it is for the tranquillity of the inhabitants to know minutely the occupation of the negroes, their numerical distribution in the sugar estates, farms, and cities. To

remedy the evil, to prevent public calamities, and to
console the unfortunate beings who belong to an ill-
treated race, and who are feared more than is
acknowledged, it is necessary to probe the sore; for
there exists in social, as well as organic bodies,
reparative forces, which, when well directed, may
triumph over the most inveterate evils.

In 1811, when the Ayuntamiento and the *Consu-
lado* estimated the total population of the island at
600,000, of which 326,000 were colored, free and
slave; the distribution of this mass of negroes,
between the towns and the rural districts, showed
the following results, comparing each partial number with the whole number of blacks, considered as
a unit:

Western department.	Free.	Slave.	Total.
In towns,	11	11½	22½
In rural districts,	1½	34	35½
Eastern department.			
In towns,	11	9½	20½
In rural districts,	11	10½	21½
	34½	65½	100

It appears, from this table, which may be subject
to correction by subsequent investigations, that, in
1811, nearly three-fifths of the blacks resided in the
district of Havana, between Cape San Antonio and
Alvarez; that, in that part of the island, there were

as many free negroes as slaves, but that the total colored population of the towns, compared with that of the country, was as 2 to 3. On the other hand, in the eastern portion of the island, from Alvarez to St. Jago de Cuba, the number of blacks living in the towns was nearly equal to that in the country.[1]

We shall see, further on, that between the years 1811 and 1825, Cuba received, through licit and illicit channels, 185,000 African negroes, of which nearly 116,000 were entered at the custom-house of Havana, between 1811 and 1820. This recently imported mass has undoubtedly been distributed more in the country than in the towns, and will have affected the estimated proportions which well-

[1] This disposition of the free blacks to abandon the rural districts, and gather in the towns, is very striking, and worthy of careful study by social economists. The form of the latest census returns in Cuba, does not enable us to institute the exact comparison here made by Baron Humboldt; but that of 1846 shows that the city of Havana and suburbs, contained the following proportions of the total population of the Western department :

	White.	Free Col'd.	Slaves.
Havana,...................	39	51	11
Rest of department, ...	71	49	39

It would be interesting to know if the same tendency to abandon the rural districts exists among the free negroes of St. Domingo and Jamaica, and, if so, what effect it has upon their social and moral condition.

informed persons had ascertained in 1811, as existing between the eastern and western parts of the island, and the country and towns. · The slaves have increased largely in the eastern districts, but the fearful certainty that, notwithstanding the importation of 185,000 new negroes, the mass of free colored and slaves, mulattoes and blacks, had increased only 64,000, or one-fifth, between 1811 and 1825, exhibits clearly that the changes experienced by the relations of partial distribution, are reduced to much narrower limits than might have been supposed.

Supposing the population, as already stated, to be 715,000 (which I believe to be within the minimum number), the ratio of population in Cuba, in 1825, is 197 individuals to the square league, and, consequently, nearly twice less than that of St. Domingo, and four times smaller than that of Jamaica. If Cuba were as well cultivated as the latter island, or, more properly speaking, if the density of population were the same, it would contain 3515 × 874 or 3,159,000 inhabitants;[1] that is to say, more than are

[1] Supposing the population of Haiti to be 820,000, it is 334 persons to the square league, and if we estimate it at 936,000, it is 382. Native writers suppose the island of Cuba to be capable of maintaining seven and two-sevenths millions of inhabitants. (See Remonstrance of the Cuban Deputies, against the tariff of 1821, p. 9.)

now contained in the Republic of Colombia, or in all the archipelago of the Antilles. Yet Jamaica has 1,914,000 acres of waste land.

The most remote official census and statistics that I could obtain, during my residence in Havana, are those of 1774 and 1775, compiled by order of the Marquis de la Torre, and that of 1791, by order of Don Luis de las Casas.' Everyone is aware that both these were made with great negligence, and a large part of the population was omitted. The census of 1775, which is known as that of the Abbé Raynal, gives the following figures:

Even under this hypothesis, the ratio of population would not be equal to that of Ireland.—H.

' This governor was the founder of the Patriotic Society, the Board of Agriculture and Trade, the Chamber of Commerce, the Orphan Asylum, the Chair of Mathematics, and several primary schools. He intended to ameliorate the barbarous forms of criminal law, and created the noble office of advocate for the poor. The improvement and ornament of the city of Havana, the building of the highway to Guanajay, the construction of docks, the protection afforded to writers for the press, that they might give vigor to public spirit, all date from his time. Don Luis de las Casas y Aragorri, captain-general of Cuba (1790-1796), was born in the village of Sopuerta, in Biscay ; he fought with great distinction in Portugal, at Pensacola, in the Crimea, before Algiers, at Mahon, and at Gibraltar. He died in July, 1800, at Puerto Santa Maria, at the age of 65 years. See the compendiums of his life by friar Juan Gonzalez, and by Don Tomas Romay.—H.